Business Renewal and Performance in Jamaica

Business Renewal and Performance in Jamaica

WILLIAM W. LAWRENCE

THE UNIVERSITY OF THE WEST INDIES PRESS

Jamaica • Barbados • Trinidad and Tobago

The University of the West Indies Press
7A Gibraltar Hall Road, Mona
Kingston 7, Jamaica
www.uwipress.com

A catalogue record of this book is available from the National Library of Jamaica.

978-976-640-498-7 (print)
978-976-640-535-9 (Kindle)
978-976-640-539-7 (ePub)

Cover design by Robert Harris
Typesetting by The Beget, India
Printed in the United States of America

Contents

Preface

Why are some firms able to recover from the adverse effects of external pressures and internal weaknesses while others perish? Business literature continues to seek the elusive answer to that question. This book is a milestone in a journey that I began more than two decades ago as a businessman and scholar intent on providing managerial guidance on how to rescue struggling but potentially viable companies from losses and insolvency. Along the way, I saw Jamaican organizations subjected to profound environmental jolts such as the liberalization of trade and exchange controls in 1991, the financial sector crisis in the late 1990s, and the global economic crisis from 2007 to 2009.

The fact that several entities were able to weather the negative impacts of these challenges raises some vitally important questions for research. How can firms recognize the early warning signs of impending performance decline? What are the available options for resolving financial crisis? How should managers select and execute turnaround strategies? What is the best way to increase operational efficiency? This book provides perspectives from a new lens – a simple, yet highly effective set of turnaround pathways developed from a sharp review of international literature and exploration of the business models of Jamaican firms.

The chapters of the book form a practical toolkit for use by company directors, business managers, entrepreneurs, national policymakers, attorneys-at-law, academics, students, educational institutions and others. This book may be adopted either as a stand-alone text or as a complement to other written materials in the fields of business policy, general management, strategy, entrepreneurship and finance. I am deeply indebted to close colleagues, friends and family for their valuable contributions in turning my vision of publishing this book into reality.

William W. Lawrence

Acknowledgements

This book is dedicated to my family and sources of inspiration Marcia, Raymond, Brian and Kathryn. I thank almighty God and all others who have made this book a reality. Thanks to the staff at Mona School of Business and Management at the University of the West Indies, especially the hardworking team in the Professional Services Unit. Special thanks to Patricia Douce and Ingrid Bennett for proofreading the manuscript. I thank the University of the West Indies Press for publishing my work and the three international reviewers for useful comments and suggestions.

1 | The Challenge of Business Renewal

Business renewal is a neglected topic of discussion and education in Jamaica despite substantial evidence of corporate losses and widespread financial hardship among small ventures. From the perspective of turnaround management, business renewal is the process of regaining pre-downturn levels of company profitability and financial health following a period of declining performance (Hofer, 1980; Schendel, Patton & Riggs, 1976). This transformation involves planned or emergent changes in organizational priorities, arrangements and activities to make a firm better suited to its environment (Weilemaker, Elfring, & Volberda, 2000).

Contrary to public expectations, from 1992 to 2012, company income tax as a percentage of total taxes fell from 11.7 per cent to 7.8 per cent. The number of small firms filing returns for General Consumption Tax declined from 18,142 in 2005, to 10,447 in 2012 (Planning Institute of Jamaica, 2006 and 2013). Lower tax contributions adversely affect national wealth accumulation and become a problem for countries like Jamaica where real growth of gross domestic product (GDP) lags behind the world average.

Results from a global survey conducted by PricewaterhouseCoopers (2013) indicated that companies in Latin America and the Caribbean demonstrate high risk factors of business failure. Data from firms publicly listed on the main market of the Jamaica Stock Exchange supports these findings. Of the eighty-four firms listed since inception of the stock exchange in 1969, forty-seven have reported losses, and only twenty-five of these survived (table 1.1). Companies from all business sectors experienced losses at different points in time, and even large conglomerates having multiple revenue streams felt the sting of the downturn.

Jamaica has a long history of high-profile corporate failures. In the 1970s, Bryden and Evelyn, a leading merchandise distributor, collapsed after losing control of its accounts receivables. During the 1980s, Kingston Industrial Works, a major metal fabricator, ceased operations because of reduced revenues from its main source, the ailing manufacturing sector. In the 1990s, conglomerate Industrial Commercial Developments relied too heavily on debt financing and became insolvent when interest rates rose sharply. During the first decade of the twenty-first century, Island Life Insurance Company was closed because of a mismatch in the maturities of its assets and liabilities.

Manufacturing firms and financial institutions account for roughly half of all firms listed on the Jamaica Stock Exchange. Most of the losses in the manufacturing sector occurred in the 1990s after Jamaica liberalized trade and foreign exchange controls in order to open the local market. Import duties were reduced, and competition from foreign products became more intense. Rising interest rates and currency devaluation made production costs untenable for firms heavily dependent on the domestic market. Several subsidiaries of foreign based multinational corporations relocated to other countries.

In the late 1990s, the government established the Financial Sector Adjustment Company Limited (FINSAC) to rescue local financial institutions from

Table 1.1. Firms Listed on the Jamaica Stock Exchange Main Market (1969–2012)

Business Area	Listed	Decline	Recovery
Manufacturing	23	17	9
Financial services	20	4	2
Insurance and real estate	9	4	2
Conglomerate	9	4	2
Mass communications	5	4	3
Trading	5	3	2
Hospitality	4	4	2
Gaming and entertainment	4	3	2
Utilities and transportation	3	3	1
Storage	2	1	0
Total Firms	84	47	25

Source: Jamaica Stock Exchange yearbooks.

widespread liquidity problems due to rising numbers of bad debts and severe cash flow challenges. Real estate properties which were overvalued during this period of high inflation were often used to guarantee bank loans. Weaknesses in financial regulations and risk management were exposed when the Government of Jamaica took anti-inflationary measures. FINSAC was financed through borrowing from the domestic market to protect depositors through intervention, rehabilitation and then divestment of various financial institutions.

Studies show that small businesses also struggle in the current economic climate. In fact, few small companies survive beyond ten years in business. (Lawrence, 2012). Owners/managers are concerned about pressure from currency devaluation, economic recession, competition and onerous taxation. Welsh and White (1981) mention that small businesses may be even more susceptible to failure because of their inherently different structures compared to large corporations. They note that "a small business is not a little big business" because resource deficiency and limited revenue streams make the smaller firm more vulnerable to environmental jolts than their larger counterparts. In light of the attrition of large and small businesses, the Global Entrepreneurship Monitor (2010), accurately calls for a greater emphasis to be placed on business growth and a reduction of business discontinuation.

Global Hardships

The harsh business climate in Jamaica reflects realities consequent to the 2007–2008 global economic crisis regarded by some economists as the worst since the Great Depression of the 1930s (Planning Institute of Jamaica, 2009). This crisis created liquidity shortfalls in banking systems around the world that triggered substantial contractions in credit and international trade. A changed environment, called "the new normal", emerged, containing features such as more volatile consumer demand and heightened competition (Butler, Atkins & Ivester, 2010). These conditions have created a greater propensity for business failure because of downward pressure on revenue streams.

As a result of the new economic environment, several large multinational corporations became bankrupt. General Motors posted a record loss of $38 billion for 2007 and offered buyouts to all seventy-four thousand of its unionized employees in a bid to reduce costs. This drastic decline occurred due to a substantial slowing of the motor vehicle market. General Motors introduced an early retirement programme and a cash buy-out scheme in exchange for post-retirement healthcare benefits. However, the company continued to lose market share, prompting the US Federal government to intervene and purchase 500 million shares, or about 26 per cent of the company.

Similarly, the Netherlands financial giant ABN Amro incurred losses due to a subsequent downturn of the Dutch economy and loan default by the Greek government. The Dutch government rescued the bank in 2008 to the tune of nearly 40 billion euros and later acknowledged that its plan to divest ABN Amro in 2014 was unlikely to be profitable. This action undoubtedly increased the financial burden on taxpayers.

Additionally, Canadian phone equipment maker, Nortel Networks, fell victim to reduced spending by customers and intensified competition from foreign companies. As a result, the company incurred substantial losses, and its share price fell by 69 per cent on the Toronto Stock Exchange. Nortel filed for bankruptcy protection and held financial obligations to about twenty-five thousand creditors. In the United Kingdom, losses at the Royal Bank of Scotland widened amid declining revenues and rising costs due in part to regulatory violations. The bank was also troubled with other legal issues such as allegedly fixing the Libor, a key interbank lending rate.

These cases illustrate how environmental shifts can trigger substantial erosion of a companies' financial health. In order to affect turnaround from recessive situations, companies must transition to a new business model; however, this can be a difficult adjustment to make (Miles, 2010). A global survey by McKinsey and Company revealed that less than 40 per cent of all corporate transformations are successful (Isern, Meaney & Wilson, 2010). The success rate for offensive or proactive transformations is 47 per cent compared to 34 per cent for defensive or reactive transformations. This is bad news for firms in Jamaica that are already hard hit by declining world prices for commodities and the removal of preferential access to markets overseas.

Macroeconomic Pressures

Economic growth and the creation of employment opportunities are major goals of the Government of Jamaica. To this end, the country pursues the implementation of policies known collectively as the Washington Consensus (the enforcement of property rights, maintenance of macroeconomic stability, integration with the world economy, and creation of a sound business environment). However, Jamaica, like other small island developing states, is constrained by its small domestic market, few sources of national income and employment, susceptibility to natural disasters, propensity for brain-drain which undermines productivity, limited power in global relations, and difficulties in competing globally and attracting foreign capital (Elliott & Palmer, 2008).

Data from the Planning Institute of Jamaica, over the period 2003 to 2012, show that real growth of GDP averaged only 0.3 per cent per annum compared to the 3.9 per cent world average GDP. The country has trade deficits every year and relies heavily on borrowed funds and debt rescheduling. According to the World Development Report (2010), Jamaica is one of the slowest growing countries in the Caribbean Common Market (CARICOM) as well as one of the slowest growing low/middle income countries globally. Jamaica also continues to be among the least competitive countries in the world based on annual surveys conducted by the World Economic Forum.

In 2007, the Government of Jamaica launched a long-term strategic plan called "Vision 2030 Jamaica" aimed at making the country the place of choice to live, work, raise families and do business through a set of economic, social, environmental and governance initiatives (Planning Institute of Jamaica, 2013). However, Jamaica's economic and social environment continues to be very weak on key indicators such as real growth of GDP, currency stability and employment levels (table 1.2).

A weakened economy adversely affects company revenues because of lower consumer spending power. Thus, collecting accounts receivable becomes more difficult, and bad debts tend to rise. Companies often find it difficult to scale back operations, even after downsizing staff, because of fixed costs embedded in existing infrastructure and long-term contractual commitments. This situation worsened in Jamaica, following the removal of trade and exchange controls by

Table 1.2. Selected Jamaica Economic and Social Statistics

Indicator	2005–6	2008–9	2011–12
Real GDP growth	1.9%	-2.0%	0.5%
Inflation rate	11.8%	15.8%	7.2%
Treasury Bill yield	12.9%	20.7%	6.8%
Exchange (J$:US$1.00)	$64.29	$80.71	$87.54
Unemployment rate	10.8%	11.0%	13.2%
Major crime rate (per 100,000)	289	405	398

Source: Planning Institute of Jamaica Social and Economic Surveys.

the government in 1991, to reduce the level of protection of local firms from international competition.

Admittedly, in the years following Jamaica's independence in 1962, some companies reaped profits from preferential access to export markets at favourable prices and high tariff protection from international competition. However, these benefits have been largely eliminated. The real sectors of the economy, such as manufacturing, agriculture and mining, have contracted and Jamaica's public debt has escalated. Currency devaluation remains a big challenge for many companies that are unable to increase market prices.

Industry Decline

Several Jamaican industries have buckled under the weight of company losses and insolvency. Alcan, Kaiser and Alcoa are among the list of prominent multinational corporations that have cut back or withdrawn operations from the bauxite mining industry in Jamaica. The wood furniture industry has not yet recovered from the demise of its leading companies: Kingston Heirlooms, McIntosh Furniture and Madon. Nor has the local apparel industry come to grips with the shock of plant closures by Jockey International and Sara Lee Corporation.

National statistics, published in the annual social and economic surveys of the Planning Institute of Jamaica, show the negative economic impact of these industry contractions. In 2011, mining and quarrying contributed a mere 1.9 per cent of total GDP down from 8.7 per cent in 1976. Manufacturing and processing fell from 17.5 per cent to 8.1 per cent over the same period, while the agriculture sector contracted from 7.9 per cent to only 5.8 per cent.

Interestingly, although Jamaica has become increasingly oriented towards services, the manufacturing sector still explains nearly 40 per cent of the variation in real growth of GDP. However, the sector has been declining since the liberalization of trade and foreign exchange controls in 1991 (see figure 1.1). Manufacturers have complained about high interest rates. The weighted average interest rate on bank loans skyrocketed from 21 per cent in 1991 to nearly 50 per cent by year end 1995, while the exchange rate for the US dollar depreciated from J$14.33 to J$35.54. Financial distress became widespread in the sector because of variable interest rate loan contracts and foreign currency denominated debt acquired primarily for purchasing raw materials.

There was also an exodus of foreign-based manufacturing firms with the number of companies listed on the Jamaica Stock Exchange, contracting from

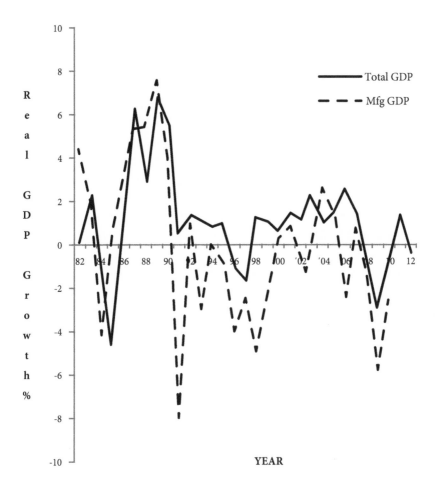

Regression of total GDP growth on manufacturing GDP growth:
$R = .62$; $R^2 = .38$; $n = 31$; F-Ratio = 16.3; $p = .000$

Figure 1.1. Jamaican manufacturing relative to total gross domestic product growth
Source: Planning Institute of Jamaica annual reports.

fifteen in the 1970s to only seven by 2011. Yet, several firms did not have the option of ceasing operations because of personal guarantees held by secured creditors. Many of these companies resorted to downsizing as a strategy to boost operational efficiency. Jobs were lost, and the level of unemployment in Jamaica would have been much higher if the government had not ramped up its intake of employees. High rates of interest, onerous taxation, high electricity costs, low capacity utilization, low value-added, high labour costs, excessive waste, uncompetitive technology and weak export activities are often cited among reasons for company performance decline.

The small business sector, regarded as the main engine for job creation, has a high rate of closure because of financial hardship. According to the Global Entrepreneurship Monitor (GEM) (2010), Jamaica has one of the highest rates of business start-ups in the world – even ahead of China and the United States. Yet, GEM also notes that fewer start-ups are becoming established businesses, and the rate of business discontinuation has increased due mainly to financial hardships. More than half of all small businesses do not survive beyond ten years.

Losses and other financial problems account for 64 per cent of small business closures. Studies also show that the likelihood of failure increases as the small business matures due to hardships that arise from inefficient operations and limited revenue streams (Lawrence, 2012). Small firms in Jamaica must also cope with input price pressures from high rates of interest on bank loans and local currency depreciation. In addition to the negative economic impact of these closures, potential new jobs are lost because successful small- and medium-sized enterprises tend to hire more people over time.

Company Losses

In 2010, National Meats and Foods, a large distributor to Jamaican wholesalers and the local hotel industry, downsized its workforce by over two hundred employees in light of company losses and pressure from creditors. Ironically, in earlier years, this company was lauded for excellent leadership, rapid expansion and modern facilities. Following a period of impressive expansion, another large corporation, Super Plus Food Stores closed several retail outlets and cut back its staffing in an attempt to halt losses. Furthermore, perpetual losses forced Caribbean Cement Company (2010) to breach its debt covenants with creditors. Cable and Wireless Jamaica (2012) continued to incur losses while being embroiled in a battle for market share with its main rival, Digicel.

Interestingly, similar patterns of expansion and loss exist within several state-owned enterprises. Jamaica Urban Transit Company had a fleet of about five hundred buses on the roads in 1999. By 2007, this number was cut in half because the company had no cash for repairs and incurred huge losses each month. The Sugar Company of Jamaica had a loss of J$1.1 billion in 2005, despite selling 130,000 tonnes of sugar; the company projected further losses

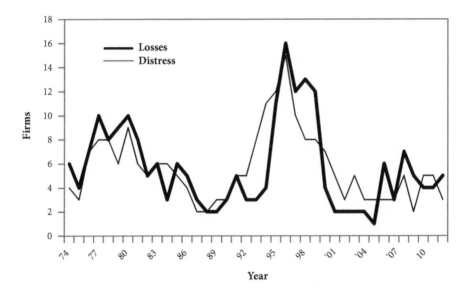

Figure 1.2. Loss-making and distressed firms on Jamaica Stock Exchange, 1974–2012
Source: Jamaica Stock Exchange yearbooks.

for 2006. Although the Government of Jamaica gave Air Jamaica an annual subsidy of US$30 million, the airline still accumulated losses of US$1.2 billion by 2009. The National Water Commission was profitable in 2000 but reported accumulated losses of J$8.5 billion by year-end March 2009.

Business renewal is quite challenging in Jamaica because company losses are often accompanied by financial distress or cash crises (figure 1.2). The losses increase dramatically in periods of economic recession, such as during the oil crises of the 1970s, and after the Jamaican government's liberalization of trade and foreign exchange controls in 1991. However, recession, measured as negative real growth of GDP, explained only 18 per cent of the variability in reported losses during the period 1974 to 2011. This suggests that most company losses are not caused by economic recession.

Foundations of Business Renewal

The process of business renewal involves modifying administrative systems and decision processes to improve company performance. In an effort to understand this management practice, scholarly research can be traced to the seminal work of Adam Smith (1977), who posited that competition regulates the economic activities of markets to allocate resources efficiently and bring about the greatest prosperity. The implications are that firms in profit trouble can reverse decline by finding ways to offer attractive prices. Frederick Taylor (1911) introduced scientific management as a means to increase company efficiency through a set of rules for redesigning work processes and methods to eliminate waste, a critical requirement for business renewal.

Barnard (1938) defined formal organizations as systems of consciously coordinated activities involving two or more persons cooperating willingly for the effective pursuit of a common purpose using appropriate communication and efficient inducements. Herbert Simon (1957) extended this work to recognize that organizations are complex networks of processes making decisions that are good enough, termed "satisficing", because individuals have bounded rationality or limited ability to grasp the present and anticipate the future. Both Barnard and Simon underscored the importance of having communications and incentives for business renewal.

Cyert and March (1963) built on the foundation laid by Simon to posit that successful organizations satisfy goals and expectations by making adaptively rational decisions about price, output and internal resource allocation. Firms prioritize goals to resolve any potential conflict. Imperfections in resource allocation create surplus or organizational slack, which enables a firm to withstand environmental jolts and search for solutions to problems. Henry Mintzberg (1994) noted that strategy may not be planned but instead emerges from random managerial actions or learning from trial and error. These ideas highlight the importance of having a cushion of resources in the event of errors during business renewal (Lawrence, 1995).

Burns and Stalker (1961) and Lawrence and Lorsch (1967) put forward the contingency theory to describe the organization as an open system operating in a state of dynamic equilibrium with the environment. This system works best when there is harmony in the exchanges of goods, services, information and resources. However, this equilibrium can be disrupted by adverse shifts in the environment that trigger declining performance. For survival, a firm must choose the appropriate corrective action or strategy that is contingent on the peculiarities of its situation. Firms planning for business renewal need to consider not only content and process but also the environmental context.

Several scholars have made important contributions to the literature on business turnaround. Gopinath (1991) wrote that delay in decline recognition induces external agents to intervene and influence strategic decisions sometimes to the detriment of the troubled firms. Looking at business renewal as corporate turnaround or recovery from profit decline, Schendel, Patton and Riggs (1976) analysed data on fifty-four US-based manufacturing firms and concluded that turnaround most often comes from regaining efficiency or changing strategy, depending on the cause of the decline. O'Neill (1986) noted that the prescriptions put forward by Schendel, Patton and Riggs (1976) were also relevant for commercial banks. Ramanujam (1984) observed that turnaround unfolds in phases.

Hofer (1980) argued that turnaround is only worth attempting if the going concern value of a firm is substantially greater than its liquidation value. Managers can use bankruptcy prediction models to decide whether or not business failure is imminent. Wruck (1990) proposed that financial distress, which he terms cash flow–based insolvency, is the critical determinant of business failure rather than stock-based insolvency, where total liabilities exceed total assets. According to Lawrence (2001), firms experiencing financial distress must use either private workouts or bankruptcy reorganization to defer, shrink or transfer debt obligations to affordable levels. Workouts are faster but bankruptcy petitions offer more protection.

Robbins and Pearce (1992) argued that retrenchment, defined as cutbacks in costs or assets, is a necessary component of all successful turnarounds. However, Barker and Mone (1994) and Arogyaswamy and Yasai-Ardekani (1996) disagreed based on data showing that some turnarounds occurred without retrenchment but instead through sales growth. Barker and Duhaime (1997) noted that firms must take industry and firm-variables into account when changing strategy. Lawrence (2004) revealed that shareholders can use perceptions of risk, measured as volatility in earnings per share, to determine whether or not turnaround is actually taking place.

Roadmap for Business Renewal

Although the literature on business renewal is abundant, there is need to articulate a cohesive set of steps to guide managerial decisions for recovery from organizational decline (Francis & Desai, 2005). The case studies described in the literature infer collectively that the process of business renewal involves the following steps.

1. *Recognize the severity and source of organizational decline.* Gopinath (1991) noted that recognition involves management's admission of the

problem and commitment to business renewal. Lorange and Nelson (1987) argued that decline often follows a period of success because of managerial complacency which can be recognized by amplifying warning signals such as incompetence, excess personnel, bureaucracy and self-deception. This requires vigilance and prompt corrective action to avert worsening or spreading of the problems (Thain & Goldthorpe, 1989a).

2. *Resolve financial distress where necessary.* Firms need to resolve issues of financial distress quickly or they will likely cease to exist (Winn, 1989). Hofer (1980) remarked that turnaround is only worth attempting if the going concern value of a firm is substantially greater than its liquidation value. Altman and La Fleur (1981) observed that the sale of non-core and idle assets can provide cash for debt reduction.

3. *Change strategy if required.* O'Neill (1986) found that firms changed management, cut back, grew or restructured business portfolios depending on the cause of the problem. Schendel, Patton and Riggs (1976) observed that corporate strategy was changed if the source of the problem was external environmental pressures. However, strategy should remain unchanged if the source comes from internal weaknesses such as waste. Barker and DuHaime (1997) concluded that the extent of strategic change depends on industry dynamics and a firm's ability to change.

4. *Increase operations efficiency.* Lawrence (2008) noted that there are several ways to increase efficiency depending on the scope and scale of output as well as the state of resource inputs, such as levels of waste and technological sophistication. Arogyaswamy and Yasai-Ardekani (1996) observed that some firms were able to achieve turnaround without increasing efficiency. Turnaround occurred in these cases as a result of cutbacks in employees and positive trends in accounts receivable, inventory and company expenses.

5. *Sustain the performance recovery.* Higgins (1977) argued that the maximum annual increase in sales that a firm can afford depends on its available financial resources. To avoid financial hardship, firms need to keep sales growth within limits that can be supported by available resources. Early decline recognition is also critical to spot and avert potential erosion of resources (Lorange & Nelson, 1987).

These steps form the major set of activities in a turnaround and take time for completion. Table 1.3 shows the turnaround profiles of four Jamaican companies based on these steps.

Courts Jamaica, a retailer of home furnishings and appliances, was the local market leader for many years; however, rivals such as Homelectrix offered lower prices rendering Courts uncompetitive and causing it to lose its position in the market. In 1995, the company was jolted into action after two years of profit decline with losses. The company used its substantial financial reserves to open additional branches across the island, widen the range of products, upgrade its technology to improve operational efficiency and offer the lowest prices and the

Table 1.3. Business Renewal at Four Firms in Jamaica

	Courts Jamaica	Gleaner Company	Salada Foods	Desnoes and Geddes
Industry	Home furnishings	Mass media	Coffee	Beverage
Duration of decline	2 years	3 years	4 years	3 years
Source of decline	Complacency	High costs	Productivity	Competition
Severity of decline	Losses	Losses	Losses and cash crisis	Losses and cash crisis
Financial restructuring	None	None	Sale of assets; Rights issue; Refinancing	Sale of assets; Rights issue
Strategic change	None	Sold Sangster's Book Store	None	Sold wines, spirits, and soft drinks business units
Efficiency increase	Added products and branches; upgraded inventory technology	Reduced waste in operations; new circulation technology	Staff cut-back; more distributors	Exports; staff cutback; upgraded plant technology
Time for recovery	3 years	2 years	6 years	3 years

most attractive credit terms in the industry. Courts increased sales substantially to reverse the decline and recapture market share by 1998.

Newspaper kingpin, the Gleaner Company, had grown appreciably through selective acquisitions in Jamaica and overseas. However, rising costs outpaced revenue growth from 2005 to 2008. Consequently, the company cut back assets by selling a loss-making subsidiary, Sangster's Book Stores, to stem losses and to get cash needed to upgrade its equipment. This strategic move, executed over two years, enabled the Gleaner to refocus on its core business of media and to regain profitability, although revenues remained flat.

During the early 1990s, Salada Foods, producers of instant coffee, had an inefficient supply chain that affected its productivity. The company incurred losses and had a severe cash crisis by 1995. To effect turnaround, Salada Foods had a rights issue of shares, sold a loss-making investment initiative overseas, refinanced debt at more favourable terms, cut back staffing and increased the number of distributors. By 2001, the company had regained financial health and resumed a path of robust revenue growth.

Desnoes and Geddes entered the decade of the 1990s as the dominant producer of alcoholic and non-alcoholic beverages. However, price competition became very intense in the aftermath of the liberalization of trade and exchange controls. The company plunged into losses and financial distress by 1995. Turnaround took three years to achieve and involved selling non-core assets, disinvesting in soft drinks and non-brewed alcoholic business units, expanding in export markets, cutting staff and upgrading plant equipment.

Ultimately, while Courts Jamaica relied only on efficiency improvements by expanding its infrastructure and range of output, Salada Foods and Desnoes and Geddes used a combination of asset retrenchment and debt restructuring to resolve the cash crisis. The Gleaner Company and Desnoes and Geddes each changed their business strategies to mitigate pressure from external sources of decline. All four firms took actions to increase efficiency albeit in different ways. The organizational behaviour patterns of these four companies translate logically to a high-level turnaround roadmap for achieving business renewal.

For any viable firm, the correct route depends on the answers to three questions in sequence (see figure 1.3). First, is the company currently in a cash crisis? If so, financial restructuring is necessary. Second, is the source of decline external to the company? An affirmative answer necessitates a change of strategy. Third, is performance recovery taking place? If not, the attempt at turnaround must be repeated and perhaps through a different set of actions. Firms should strive to achieve turnaround on the first attempt because each failed

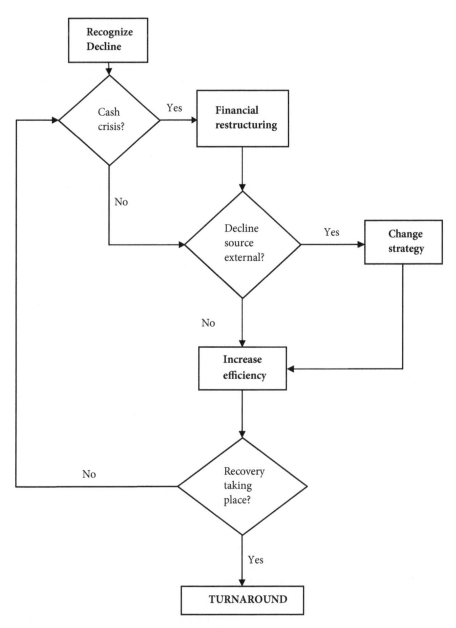

Figure 1.3. A roadmap for business renewal

effort consumes resources which further weakens the company. This does not mean that turnaround is an event that happens overnight. Each of the four Jamaican cases described achieved business renewal only after several years of dedicated effort to the process. However, managers need to deploy resources in the most effective and efficient ways to avoid any need for restarting the turn-around cycle.

Managers can track the progress of turnaround by using financial ratios (Winn, 1989). These metrics are also important for understanding the phases of decline and recovery and examining the utility of strategic initiatives (Pearce, 2007). The information contained in company annual reports is also useful in distinguishing between declining firms that achieve turnaround and those that fail (Smith & Graves, 2005). As the turnaround process unfolds, there is an overlapping transition from the decline-stemming phase for halting the down-turn, to the recovery phase that restores performance to pre-downturn levels (Lawrence, 2011).

The shape of the turnaround cycle reflects the degree of turnaround dif-ficulty. A V-shaped cycle occurs when the performance decline is not severe and the company has sufficient resources to develop and execute the correct turnaround plan in a timely manner. The turnaround cycle becomes U-shaped when a firm undergoes financial restructuring and has difficulty executing the plan for performance recovery. Courts Jamaica and the Gleaner Company had V-shaped turnaround cycles because neither firm was in financial distress and had cash at hand to fuel quick recovery (figure 1.4). Desnoes and Geddes had a U-shaped cycle because of financial restructuring and challenges arising from its transition from a family-owned business to a subsidiary of a foreign-based multinational corporation.

A W-shaped cycle, similar to that of Salada Foods, emerges when a firm has difficulty with financial restructuring and the initial attempt at turnaround fails to achieve recovery. National Commercial Bank (NCB) incurred losses and liquidity problems when its portfolio of client bad debts rose to abnormal lev-els during a period of very high interest rates in Jamaica. NCB's initial attempt at turnaround, using its own resources, failed to resolve the problem, and the institution subsequently received liquidity support from the government under the FINSAC programme. As a consequence, the turnaround cycle of NCB was W-shaped or erratic which is sometimes called non-monotonic .

Courts Jamaica and Salada Foods are examples of operating turnaround that requires no change of corporate or business strategy. The Gleaner Company and Desnoes and Geddes achieved strategic turnaround by making necessary adjustments to their business portfolios. Business renewal takes time to achieve and can occur even during economic recession as was the case for Courts Jamaica, the Gleaner Company and Desnoes and Geddes.

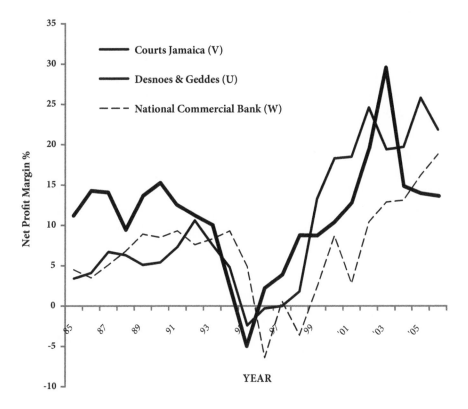

Figure 1.4. V, U and W-shaped turnaround cycles
Source: Jamaica Stock Exchange yearbooks.

Managers should avoid premature declarations of success. A return to pre-downturn levels of performance does not mean automatically that the recovery will be sustained. Workers Bank announced "mission accomplished", in the company's 1994 annual report, but the organization collapsed just two years later. Furthermore, a firm may undergo more than one turnaround cycle during its lifetime. Salada Foods had a turnaround cycle from 1979 to 1989 and another one from 1993 to 2002.

Further Evidence

The utility of the roadmap is further illustrated by comparing and contrasting how two similar manufacturing firms, KIW Group, a fabricator of metal products, and CMP Industries, a producer of metal products and electrical wires, attempted turnaround (figure 1.5). During the 1970s both firms incurred losses because of the negative impact of the global oil crisis on the manufacturing sector. Non-oil commodity prices fell sharply while the cost of electricity and petrol-based transportation rose substantially. KIW Group cut staff and tightened expense controls to increase efficiency, but they ultimately collapsed after a long period of financial distress. In contrast, CMP Industries changed their strategy by diversifying into unrelated lines of business, shoes and garment retailing, to achieve full recovery from decline.

The turnaround roadmap in figure 1.3 prescribes change of strategy for both KIW Group and CMP Industries because of the external source of decline. Yet, only the latter made the adjustment required for survival. Strategic change redefined how CMP deployed resources to interact with the new environment.

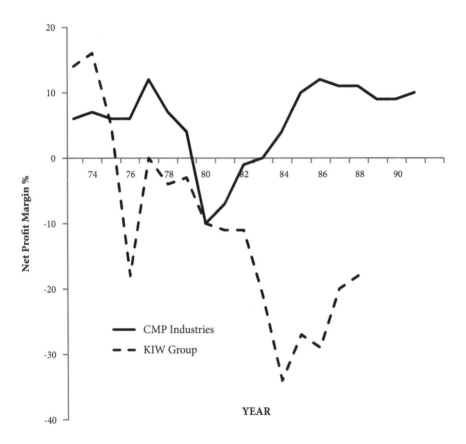

Figure 1.5. Turnaround at CMP Industries and failure at KIW Group
Source: Jamaica Stock Exchange yearbooks.

The prescriptions in the roadmap also explain the process of turnaround at other companies listed on the Jamaica Stock Exchange (table 1.4). AMG Packaging and Paper Company incurred losses because its capacity was too low to meet demand. The company upgraded its factory equipment to cope with this internal source of decline and recovered within two years. The Pegasus Hotel experienced weak demand for hotel rooms and recovered from this external source of decline by repackaging its services to offer the business community a broader and more appealing range of services.

Cinema operators, Palace Amusement Company Limited, had severe losses and financial distress because of competition from cable television. For turnaround, the company closed theatres across the island, sold real estate to repay debt, and reconfigured the remaining cinemas to give customers a choice of new

Table 1.4. Profiles of Profit Decline and Recovery at Four Jamaican Firms

	AMG Packaging	Pegasus Hotel	Palace Amusement	National Commercial Bank
Main business	Cardboard boxes	Hotel	Cinema	Banking
Number of employees	63	312	189	2,184
Decline duration	2 years	5 years	6 years	4 years
Source of decline	Limited capacity	Weak demand	Competition	Asset/liabilities mismatch
Severity of decline	Losses	Losses	Losses and cash crisis	Losses and cash crisis
Financial restructuring	None	None	Sale of assets	Sale of assets
Strategic change	None	Repackaged services	None	Refocused on banking
Efficiency increase	Upgrade equipment	Positive	Developed multi-cinemas	Upgraded technology
Time for recovery	2 years	3 years	3 years	2 years
Agrees with roadmap	Yes	Yes	Yes	Yes

multiple theatres within the same facility. Finally, a mismatch of assets and liabilities caused the Government of Jamaica to intervene at National Commercial Bank to restructure debt and sell non-core assets.

Leadership

Effective turnaround leadership is implicit in the roadmap and refers to the extent to which individuals in authority motivate stakeholders to participate willingly and harmoniously in support of firm recovery from organizational decline (Harker & Sharma, 2000). This motivation must take place at several organizational levels. Board members often become more involved in the planning process to underscore the importance and urgency of the situation. Salada Foods had an executive chairman leading the process of change. Desnoes and Geddes erected cross-functional, self-directed work teams on the factory floor, to identify, plan and execute projects for efficiency improvement. Best results are obtained when the values and attitudes of stakeholders are aligned to the critical objectives of the company. In addition to building economic capital in areas such as revenue growth and return on equity, leaders also need to garner social capital in the form of team spirit, passion, excitement, trust and fairness.

When organizational decline is severe, leaders tend to be more task-oriented and focused on actual outcomes from specified activities (Musczyk & Steel, 1998). However, in a crisis, leaders also need to be relationship-oriented and focused on inspiring others to contribute extraordinary levels of effort for turnaround. Leaders can benefit from being charismatic, demonstrating competence and stimulating new thought. Careful research and analysis can afford leaders a clear picture of the environment and the key issues that need to be addressed during renewal efforts. Effective turnaround leadership infuses employees with a positive "can-do" attitude and works in accordance with a documented plan that embodies discipline, knowledge and preparedness while also providing a credible course of action for turnaround.

The management at Desnoes and Geddes declared its intention to lower costs for better price competitiveness. Consequently, wage increases were very conservative and created industrial unrest that had to be settled at the Industrial Disputes Tribunal. However, the leaders worked tirelessly to earn employee trust and support. The turnaround plan was communicated at all levels of the organization. Cross-functional, self-managed teams were established to increase creativity and employee collaboration across departmental lines. Employees came to believe that they could question the status quo without prejudice and influence company performance. Straight talk was encouraged and workable solutions often came from the lower ranks. Pay incentives were used primarily to reinforce organizational change.

Building Stakeholder Relationships

Mary Parker Follett, in her 1924 masterpiece "Creative Experience", insisted that the human side of the organization cannot be ignored. Turnaround is not only about rebuilding economic value but also creating the organizational culture required to propel the process. Max Weber wrote five principles of bureaucracy, later translated from German to English in 1947 by A. M. Henderson and Talcott Parsons. The principles promoted effective and efficient organizational performance by instituting lines of authority, rules and standard operating procedures. Due to the high-level focus of the roadmap, the importance of the cultural issues that Weber addresses is not explicitly defined in the business renewal guidelines. However, organizational culture must be carefully managed in terms of alignment and development of structures, people and systems in order to execute the work flows and stakeholder engagements necessary for turnaround.

To manage organizational culture effectively in pursuit of business renewal, several human resource skills are important to acquire. . First, effective communication, including verbal, non-verbal, formal and informal varieties, helps to gain stakeholder commitment. Managers must be concise and accurate when sending messages, listen carefully when conversing, use body language consciously and be open to different views. Second, the ability to motivate employees to increase productivity arises from purposefully developing talent, building commitment and setting tasks that are specific, measurable, attainable, rewarding and timely. Third, when conflicts arise among stakeholders, resolution should be sought through identifying win-win outcomes using techniques such as accommodation, compromise, collaboration, avoidance or confrontation when necessary.

Finally, in order to negotiate successfully with stakeholders, managers should commit to mutual gain and strive for agreements based on objective criteria. Stress must be managed through recreational activities, proper diet, adequate preparation and teamwork. Managers need to also lead by example, cope with politics by garnering support from key stakeholders and work from a strategic plan.

The Challenge

The Government of Jamaica has implemented policies which are designed to provide additional support for the private sector such as the Micro, Small and Medium-sized Enterprise Policy and the Bankruptcy and Insolvency Act (2014). These acts seek to facilitate business renewal by way of court-supervised processes for company rehabilitation. While these policies are steps in the right direction, business leaders also need context-specific managerial guidance on how to renew their companies internally. Figure 1.3 depicts possible renewal strategies and enables managers to choose the correct pathway for their contexts. However, more detail is required to provide managers important information and tools for recognizing decline, restructuring financial contracts, changing strategy and increasing efficiency to elicit turnaround. This book provides the answer to a fundamental question: How should managers attempting business renewal achieve turnaround or recovery from organizational decline? As they say, the devil is in the details because, even after choosing the correct pathway in the roadmap, managers are challenged to navigate the specifics.

This book observes and outlines changes in company behaviour and performance over time in order to detect general patterns for informing managerial decisions and actions (Isaac & Michael, 1990). Data was extracted from company annual reports, local media releases, company website postings, the website of the Jamaica Stock Exchange, interviews with current and former company directors, and written company reports prepared by analysts at stock brokerage firms. Other sources included records prepared by the Planning Institute of Jamaica and the Bank of Jamaica.

The first chapter of this book uses this data to evolve a high-level roadmap for business renewal that is generally applicable to viable firms experiencing losses and cash flow problems. The other chapters will expand this treatment sequentially to show granular application of the roadmap to every phase of the turnaround process. The approach is both descriptive and prescriptive using a combination of statistical analysis of company data and real case studies.

Chapter 2 discusses organizational decline and shows how to recognize and assess survival-threatening erosion of organizational resources. Chapter 3 examines how to resolve financial distress and presents four strategies for boosting cash flow and reversing insolvency. Chapter 4 shows how to choose corporate-level and business-level strategies using the balanced scorecard methodology to build competitive advantage. Chapter 5 looks at how to improve operations efficiency by optimizing the scale and scope of outputs while reducing waste and leveraging technologies. Chapter 6 presents practical ideas for sustaining performance recovery through strategic foresight and effective governance. The conclusion provides a final reflection of the roadmap that summarizes and connects the main perspectives from prior chapters of the book.

2 | Recognizing Organizational Decline

Organizational decline refers to a substantial, absolute decrease in the resource base of a firm (Cameron, Kim, & Whetton, 1987). This adversity diminishes a company's ability both to withstand environmental jolts and to invest in new developmental projects (Hambrick & D'Aveni, 1988). The signs of decline may be either obscure or visible. Management at Courts Jamaica admitted that the company was complacent and unaware of early signs that a major competitor was gaining strength in the marketplace. Conversely, during organizational decline, both Salada Foods and Desnoes and Geddes noticed visible signs of working capital erosion even though revenues were increasing.

Companies enter a state of decline when they fail to anticipate, recognize, avoid, neutralize or adapt to external or internal pressures that threaten their long-term survival (Weitzel & Jonsson, 1989). Unless corrected by way of deliberate actions, resource erosion continues until the business fails. Some scholars treat decline as the final stage of the product life cycle. However, decline can occur at any stage of the cycle, including during growth if there is a mismatch between the way a firm behaves and the dictates of its environment. For example, the Jamaica Pegasus Hotel incurred overall losses although its main source of revenue, business travel, was growing at a fast pace. In contrast, Palace Amusement Company operated in the mature cinema industry and struggled not due to poor internal behaviours, but because of competition from cable television.

Another important conceptualization of decline is that it should not be confused with either turbulence or stagnation. Turbulence refers to fluctuations or instability in a firm's performance that cause outcomes to vary positively or negatively from expectations. Turbulence may occur whether or not firm performance is declining. Stagnation is a period of slow or no growth relative to some benchmark, such as past company performance or the rate of inflation in an economy. Stagnation can persist without causing significant decline as long as the stagnant firm has enough financial resources to meet its obligations.

Figure 2.1 shows a comparison of these three distinct phenomena based on trends in net profit margins over the period from1974 to 1988. Decline at KIW Group was a downward spiral because this company suffered substantial erosion of net working capital, an important indicator of the level of slack resources. Organizational slack or surplus acts as a cushion against environmental jolts and also provides funding for strategic initiatives (Cyert & March, 1963). The turbulence at Montego Bay Ice Company arose from erratic

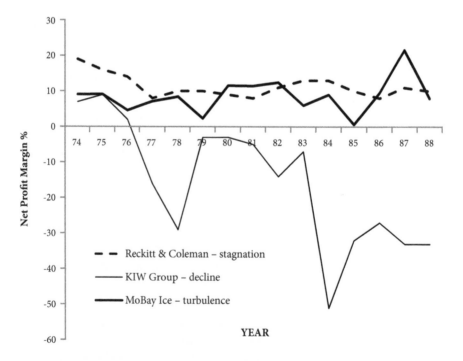

Figure 2.1. Organizational decline, turbulence and stagnation

fluctuations in organizational behaviour, but there was no visible resource erosion. Reckitt and Coleman experienced stagnant performance because the company relied only on selling mature products in the domestic market.

There was a substantial shift in the economic, social and political climate of Jamaica during this period, 1974 to 1988. Jamaica had three periods of economic recession starting with the global oil crisis in the 1970s which saw rapid decline in world bauxite prices, a commodity on which the country relied heavily for foreign exchange. The level of crime and violence escalated during the late 1970s due to bitter rivalry between the two main political parties and adversely affected the number and cost of commercial activities. Some companies ceased operations for safety reasons while others spent large sums for property protection. The country realized modest economic recovery in the late 1980s under a programme of reform, called structural adjustment, supervised by the International Monetary Fund.

Companies often mitigate adverse effects of turbulence by holding surplus or slack resources to cushion the organization. Firms may also transfer risk to another party, such as an insurance company. However, this option might not be readily available because of severe resource erosion. Small firms tend to have less organizational slack for protection against environmental jolts, than large corporations.

In terms of earnings volatility, firms incur more risk during periods of decline, a fact that has become more pronounced since the liberalization of trade and exchange controls in 1991. Table 2.1 shows the results from a statistical analysis of publicly traded companies attempting turnaround before and after 1991. After 1991, companies had lower return on assets (ROA) and higher

Table 2.1. Risk and Profitability for Jamaican Firms during Decline and Recovery Stages of the Turnaround Cycle

Stage		Pre-1991	Post-1991
Decline	Risk*	0.35	5.08
	ROA*	-0.14	-0.26
Recovery	Risk*	0.22	1.04
	ROA	0.11	0.12
Sample size		15	16

* Denotes significant difference (Mann Whitney 2-tailed, $p < .10$)

Note: There was no significant difference between goods-producing and service-oriented firms.

levels of earning volatility resulting from an attempt to adjust to higher input prices and intensified competition from imported products (Lawrence, 2004).

Warning Signals

Usually, a warning period can be identified prior to a firm's decline. For example, managers might mistakenly believe that weakening relations with suppliers are temporary misfortunes, or a company might lag behind its competitors in technology but continue to generate satisfactory profits. Consistent environmental scanning and proactive data analysis can help to detect these and other early warning signs of decline. However, studies show that recognizing these signals exist does not guarantee decline prevention. Sometimes, though warning signs are evident, decline seems inevitable because the qualitative nature of the adversities can obscure impending entropy. To avoid this blinded stage, managers must consistently assume that threat of decline exists and seek evidence to support this view and locate problem areas.

Early indicators of organizational decline are subtle and often ignored or overlooked by management (Lorange & Nelson, 1987). Examples of internal signals include resistance to change, surplus numbers of employees, tolerance of incompetence, weak communications and low employee morale. Some common external indicators of decline are shakeouts of industry players, changing consumer preferences, new legislation or natural disasters such as hurricanes. While recognizing external indicators is important, too often, managers blame external factors and ignore internal symptoms (Argenti, 1976). Refusal or inability to recognize decline at an early stage will escalate the problem.

Decline recognition involves noticing, interpreting and incorporating analyses of adverse stimuli in the decision-making process. Discerning factors of decline requires awareness of organizational change toward disorder, accepting that the present course of action no longer works and committing to correcting the situation (Gopinath, 1991). Before determining the appropriate solution, managers first need to assess the situation by measuring the severity and source of the problem.

Severity of Decline

The criticality of the downturn, in terms of the immediacy of the threat to firm survival, is called the severity of decline. Over time, this condition worsens from tolerable inconvenience to a crisis situation or imminent business failure. The latter stages are easily quantified and noticeable in routine reports such as financial statements. The speed and extent of decline depends on the harshness of the environment and the amount of slack resources available to a firm.

Gradual decline involves slow performance erosion and often occurs when management fails to adapt company strategy to changing environmental conditions. Changes in the general environment may take place due to political, economic, social, technological or legal forces. Industry-specific pressures for change can come from buyers, suppliers, rivals, new entrants or substitute products. In the early 1990s, Desnoes and Geddes and Courts Jamaica were faced with increased pressure from competitors that imported products consequent to the reduction of trade controls by the Government of Jamaica.

Contrastingly, sudden decline refers to rapid collapse of a firm and occurs typically from natural disasters or failure of high risk undertakings. In 2007, Jamaica Producers Group reported losses due to Hurricane Dean that destroyed its farms and operations. Their insurance policies were insufficient to cover the cost of the damage. The situation worsened in the following year when higher raw material costs forced the company to exit its biggest business unit. Decline can linger with a firm that remains in a state of sporadic losses even while operating at a subsistence level. This was the case with West Indies Pulp and Paper, a company that lingered in decline for over ten years before dissolution. The company lost some major customer contracts, and management accused foreign competitors of dumping tissue paper on the Jamaican market at prices below their real costs of production.

Weitzel and Jonsson (1989) identified five stages of decline in order of increasing severity. The first is called the blinded stage because the firm is unable to perceive internal or external problems that threaten long-term survival. The second is the inaction stage where, despite clear signs of declining performance, top management does not respond. The third stage is the faulty action stage where incumbent management, operating on poor diagnoses, makes wrong decisions to address the problem. Crisis is the fourth stage during which only radical change can halt the downturn. Decline becomes irreversible during the final stage where the only option is firm closure and dissolution.

National Water Commission, a statutory body of the Government of Jamaica, supplies over 90 per cent of Jamaica's total potable water supply from a network of more than 160 underground wells, over 116 river sources (via water treatment plants) and 147 springs. The company also has over 100 sewage (waste water) facilities serving about 30 per cent of the population in major towns and several housing developments. By the end of 2009, water supply accounted for 74 per cent of total revenues and sewage constituted 22 per cent. The National Water Commission was unable to account for two-thirds of its water output. Over 65 per cent of its accounts receivable were overdue while 87 per cent of long-term borrowings were denominated in foreign currency. As a result, the company incurred substantial losses and experienced financial distress (table 2.2).

If the liquidation value of a firm exceeds its going concern value, turnaround is not worth attempting and orderly closure will minimize total loss. Edward Altman (1968) introduced the Z-score formula to predict the likelihood that a firm will go bankrupt based on its financial health. Figure 2.2 shows his original formula developed from data on publicly traded manufacturing firms, plus two other models that make adjustments for private and non-manufacturing firms.

When Radio Jamaica reported losses in 1998, the company had a Z-score of 2.4 (above the threshold of 1.1) and achieved turnaround two years later (figure 2.3). On the other hand, Caribbean Steel had a Z-score of only 0.94 in 1996 (below the threshold of 1.8) and failed to recover.

To assess the severity of decline, managers should examine not only the extent of losses but also the amount of company liquidity available for funding recovery. This was the critical difference between Desnoes and Geddes and Courts Jamaica, with the former in financial distress due to an inability to pay all debts as they became due. More painful solutions are necessary for business renewal from severe decline caused by factors such as insolvency. For

Table 2.2. National Water Commission Decline (J$ million unless otherwise stated)

	2009	2000
Revenues	14,120	4,436
Profit/(loss)	(3,112)	475
Current assets	3,905	1,884
Current liabilities	4,237	1,346
Long-term debt	23,081	67
Shareholders' equity	7,032	5,872
Number of employees	2,277	2,271
Staff costs % revenues	42%	40%
Electricity % revenues	29%	17%
US dollar exchange rate (J$)	89	45

Source: National Water Commission annual reports.

Model 1. For manufacturing firms:
$Z = 1.2T_1 + 1.4T_2 + 3.3T_3 + 0.6T_4 + 1.0T_5.$
Z-scores less than 1.8 fall in the "Distress" zone

Model 2. For private firms:
$Z = 0.717T_1 + 0.847T_2 + 3.107T_3 + 0.420T_4 + 0.998T_5$
Z-scores less than 1.2 fall in the "Distress" zone

Model 3. For non-manufacturing firms
$Z = 6.56T_1 + 3.26T_2 + 6.72T_3 + 1.05T_4$
Z-scores less than 1.1 fall in the "Distress" zone

T_1 = Net working capital / total assets
T_2 = Retained earnings / total assets
T_3 = Earnings before interest and taxes / total assets
T_4 = Market value of equity / book value of total liabilities for model 1
T_4 = Book Value of equity / book value of total liabilities for models 2 and 3
T_5 = Sales/ total assets

Figure 2.2. Edward Altman Z-score models for predicting firm bankruptcy

non-financial organizations, the extent of decline may be measured as the ratio of net working capital to sales. At financial institutions, capital adequacy, the ratio of shareholders' equity to total assets, is often used to indicate the severity of decline.

Sources of Decline

Reasons for decline may be internal or external to a firm and related directly either to the demand or supply side of the business (Whittaker, 1999). Ciboney Hotel had high hopes for success in the growing Jamaican tourism industry. However, the company became insolvent after failing to generate enough revenues to cover its expenses. KIW Group, once a giant in the metal fabrication industry, was undone by general decline in local manufacturing, its main source of revenues. Kingston Ice Making Company generated sales at a brisk pace but collapsed because of over-reliance debt financing. Managers need to identify the root cause from among the symptoms, in order to choose the correct turnaround strategy. To identify the source, managers should list and check all symptoms of the problem (table 2.3). The source of decline is usually a symptom that is related to all other indicators of the problem and that begins to happen before

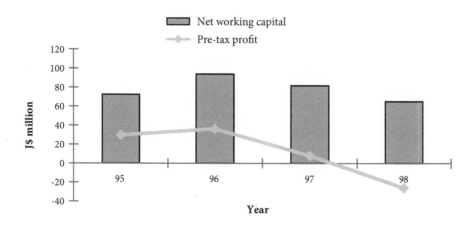

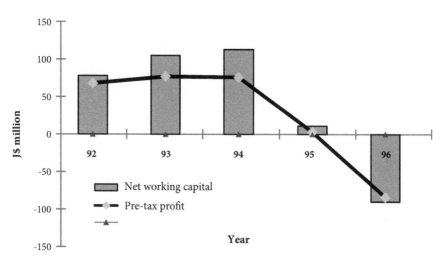

Figure 2.3. Two patterns of organizational decline

any other symptom. If none of the symptoms meet both criteria, then the search for the source of decline should continue.

Internal sources of decline are those over which management has substantial control such as overtrading, waste, uncompetitive technology and too much debt financing. Excess personnel, disproportionate staff power, tolerance of

Table 2.3. Recognizing the Source of Decline

	Internal	External
Demand	High prices Weak promotion Low product appeal	Economic recession Competition Consumer preference Natural disaster Government policy
Supply	Systems Structure Technology People Financing	Rising costs Natural disaster Government policy

incompetence, cumbersome administrative procedures, unclear communications and outdated organizational structure are early signs that something is wrong (Lorange & Nelson, 1987). External sources are environmental forces beyond the control of management, including economic recession, increasing competition, changing consumer preferences and rising input prices. Adverse changes in government policy exacerbate the level of company losses and financial distress. During the late 1970s, the Government of Jamaica implemented expenditure cutbacks and restricted foreign exchange outflows. In the mid-1990s, many firms were hurt by high interest rates and currency devaluation (figure 2.4). Many Jamaican firms purchase most of their inputs in foreign currency from overseas and the domestic market resists price increases that adjust as the Jamaican dollar devalues.

Caribbean Cement Company, a monopoly producer of cement, enjoyed robust revenue growth and profits in the early 1990s. In 1997, sales tonnage increased, but the company had a loss margin of 16 per cent and a net working capital deficit amounting to 28 per cent of total assets. Management attributed the decline to factors such as production disruptions, losses at a subsidiary company, cash loss on deposits at a local bank that went into liquidation, and the effect of the Jamaican dollar depreciation on foreign debt. A year later, the loss worsened to 68 per cent of total revenues, and the company became insolvent.

Similarly, Air Jamaica began operations in the late 1960s and expanded its routes and fleet over the next two decades. However, the airline continued to incur losses despite several revisions of its business plan, new management, company restructuring and privatization. Air Jamaica was kept alive through

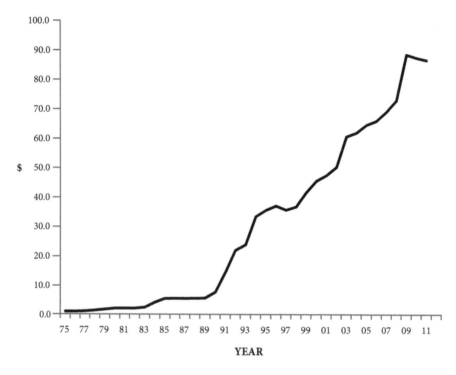

Figure 2.4. Jamaica dollar exchange rate for one US dollar

Source: Planning Institute of Jamaica Annual Economic and Social Survey (various years).

subsidies from the Government of Jamaica until the sale of its most attractive routes to Caribbean Airlines in 2010.

Internal causes of decline, such as flawed strategy or inefficiency, accounted for losses by most firms listed on the Jamaica Stock Exchange from 1974 to 2010 (table 2.4). Also, the majority of firms experiencing losses went into cash crisis or financial distress. Yet, management discussions in the company annual reports

Table 2.4. Distress and Sources of Decline for Firms on the Jamaican Stock Exchange

	External Cause	Internal Cause	Total
Distress	13	18	31
Non-distress	6	11	17
Total	19	29	**48**

Source: Company annual reports 1974–2010.

suggest that most instances of decline may have been prevented by appropriate managerial actions such as control over work processes and use of resources.

Triggers for Business Renewal

Managers sometimes contribute to organizational decline by rejecting surprising or threatening information, misinterpreting warning signals or over-indulging in groupthink while maintaining strong commitment to the current course of action (Gopinath, 2005). Such delayed recognition may also be due to fear of embarrassment, incompetence and uncertainty. Grinyer and McKiernan (1990) noted that change happens when there is sufficient dissatisfaction to create a sense of impending crisis. Managers oftentimes need to sense deep threat to spur corrective action (Schendel & Patton, 1976).

If denial persists, an influential external agent must eventually intervene to trigger change. For example, a bank may move to protect its loans at risk based on its perception of the cause of decline and the extent of client cooperation. Sometimes banks make useful suggestions regarding business strategy or even provide financial help (Gopinath, 1995). However, banks may also make the situation worse by taking legal action for debt recovery or demanding additional collateral. Other stakeholders may also intervene. Trade unions can threaten industrial action. External auditors may question a firm's ability to continue as a going concern. The media or unsecured creditors may spread negative publicity. The government can take legal action to collect overdue taxes. In turnaround situations, managers have little choice but to negotiate with influential external stakeholders for retention of control.

Should Management Be Replaced?

Organizational leaders may be replaced because of incompetence or unwillingness to embrace new ideas for change. Too often, incumbent management is reluctant to admit the problem. Thain and Goldthorpe (1989b) noted the following reasons for changing management:

- Top management was held responsible for the decline.
- A different type of leadership and experience was required.

- The change was a symbolic gesture and signalled to all stakeholders that decisive action was being taken.
- The change was punishment for management mistakes.

New management has the opportunity to correct poor employee attitudes, remove adverse coalitions of power, rekindle stakeholder support and send a clear signal to stakeholders that meaningful change is underway. Consultants are often hired to work with management to develop and execute turnaround strategies. In sum, irrespective of who is in management, delays in admitting and correcting organizational decline often results in significant financial distress.

3 | Resolving Financial Distress

The conventional perspective on downside business restructuring assumes that managers can take discretionary actions for turnaround or reversing organizational decline. However, in a situation of cash crisis, management must also negotiate with creditors to avert business failure by strengthening the company's balance sheet (Wruck, 1990). Bankruptcy re-organization and private workouts are the two primary mechanisms for resolving financial distress by reducing the debt burden to a level affordable by the restructuring firm. Bankruptcy re-organization provides legal protection against a run on assets by creditors but is costly, time consuming, and has the problem of stigma. Private workouts are faster and less costly but do not protect firms against hostile creditor actions such as receivership.

Increases in the debt to equity ratio provide an early warning signal of impending insolvency. When organizational decline becomes severe, a firm enters a state of financial distress in which monetary obligations cannot be paid as they become due. This cash deficiency, called flow-based insolvency, has to be distinguished from stock-based insolvency where total liabilities exceed total assets (Wruck, 1990). A firm may survive stock-based insolvency if there is enough cash to pay its bills but a cash-strapped entity must resolve financial distress quickly or cease to exist.

Financial distress can cause loss of market share, default on debt payments and reductions in dividend payments. Although these conditions may have arisen during a period of economic recession, waiting for economic recovery is usually not sufficient to resolve the problem. Managers must make prudent working capital decisions, liquidate assets, restructure debt or adopt a combined approach to restore financial health (Altman & La Fleur, 1981). The nature of these actions depends on the degree of firm leverage, severity of the cash crisis, ease of coordinating creditors and whether or not the economy is in a recession.

When a firm has a cash crisis, asset retrenchment and debt restructuring can shrink or defer the burden to an affordable level (Altman & La Fleur, 1981). However, the actions necessary to resolve immediate financial distress may run contrary to decisions needed for firm recovery later in the turnaround process. For example, a profitable business unit may be sold because this is the fastest way to get cash to meet urgent financial obligations. But long-term success depends on the level of support from creditors and ease of coordinating the effort for debt relief. All firms listed on the Jamaica Stock Exchange that experienced financial distress, during the period 1974 to 2010, attempted to reschedule or defer debt. Successful companies were able to divest assets, sell equity or refinance debt at lower rates of interest and over longer periods of repayment.

Desnoes and Geddes divested non-core assets such as investments in West Indies Glass Company, Antigua Brewery, Jamaica Metal Lithographers and surplus real estate. Forced sale of assets often yields only a fraction of the proceeds possible under normal market conditions, but this process may be necessary to stop cash erosion. For example, Salada Foods incurred a loss on its sale of Euro Latina Corporation after trying to use this Cuban-based subsidiary for turnaround by way of market diversification. The selling and leasing back of assets can raise money while retaining use, as was done by Caribbean Cement Company as part of its turnaround strategy in 1999.

Strategies for debt restructuring, such as rescheduling, sale of equity and refinancing, help to improve cash flow (Lawrence & Abrikian, 2013). Desnoes and Geddes and Salada Foods sold equity by way of rights issue to existing shareholders. The Government of Jamaica refinanced debt owed by Salada Foods to reduce the interest rate from 16 per cent to 12 per cent and extended the period of repayment to ten years.

The annual reports and financial statements of loss-making firms listed on Jamaica Stock Exchange, for the period 1974 to 2010, revealed that both turnaround or recovery and non-turnaround or non-recovery firms utilized a combination of strategies to relieve financial distress (table 3.1). Debt rescheduling was the most popular strategy employed by both groups. However, asset

Table 3.1. Strategies Used by Jamaican Publicly Traded Firms to Resolve Financial Distress

Strategy	Focus	Recovery Firms	Non-Recovery Firms
Total firms		23	21
Distressed firms		8	18
Reschedule	Defer debt	90% of firms	83% of firms
Retrench assets*	Shrink debt	62%	26%
Sell equity	Shrink debt	29%	13%
Refinance	Transfer debt	19%	4%

*Significant difference (Mann-Whitney two-tailed test, p < .10)

Source: Jamaica Stock Exchange yearbooks and company annual reports.

retrenchment was the only significant difference between these two groups. Firms that can retrench assets without harming core business strengths are better able to resolve financial distress. Indeed, the absence of such essential assets may be one reason for the higher rate of failure observed for small enterprises.

Managing Net Working Capital

Management of net working capital – defined as the difference between current assets and current liabilities – involves deliberate cash generation, tight control of credit limits, managed aging accounts receivable and knowledge of the terms and conditions of all payables. The cash budget becomes the central point of focus, and different scenarios should be used to anticipate risks and opportunities. The budget should also be zero-based with cash inflows sufficient to cover disbursements. This reveals whether or not turnaround plans will generate sufficient cash in a timely manner for recovery from decline. Arrangements may be made with financial institutions for new or extended lines of credit. Credit given to customers should not extend beyond the average payment cycle of the firm. Managers need to squeeze cash from accounts receivable, inventory and accounts payable. Price discounts can boost cash flows at short notice.

Asset Restructuring

If the financial performance of a company is substantially below the break-even point, managers may be able to pay down debt by selling or retrenching physical assets. Retrenchment can be challenging to execute because, in the aftermath of decline, the resource base of a firm might become badly eroded leaving few assets that can be sold without compromising the ability of the firm to continue as a going concern. Furthermore, forced sale often yields only a fraction of the cash proceeds possible under normal market arrangements. As a general rule, non-core assets should be sold as necessary in order to eliminate financial distress.

A fast way to get cash may be to sell accounts receivable to a third party such as a bank. This mechanism, called factoring, is beneficial when the rate of return of the proceeds reinvested in the business exceeds costs associated with the transaction. The extent to which such funds become available to a firm depends on the credit worthiness of the debtor and the party who is obliged to pay the invoices. Usually, the account debtor is notified of the sale, and payments are made directly to the purchaser of the accounts receivable. For positive results, the company should restrict factoring to sales over and above its break-even point. The main parts of the transaction are as follows:

1. An advance or percentage of invoice face value is paid to the seller upon submission of the invoice.
2. A reserve or remainder of total invoice amount is held until the payment is made by the account debtor.
3. A fee or cost associated with the transaction, which is deducted from the reserve before being paid back to the seller.

The bank, called the factor, may charge the seller a service fee and interest based on the waiting time to receive payments from the debtor. The factor also makes allowances for non-payment when deciding the amount to be paid to the seller.

Materials, work in progress and finish goods inventory can be sold at market or discounted prices. Dead stock may be bundled with good inventory to offer an attractive package. The Internet provides a good channel for advertising inventory for sale. However, in a turnaround situation, managers should exercise caution in giving credit. Managers should also ensure that prices, conditions and descriptions of inventory are current and correct.

Sellers of property or equipment need to have basic information available such as year, make and model, and a statement of the best features. Include clear photos and an e-mail address in advertisements. Sale and lease back may be an attractive option that would allow a firm to raise money from the sale of assets while retaining the use of them. This is an arrangement in which one party sells a property to a buyer, and the buyer immediately leases the property back to the seller. The major concerns of using this approach include increased operational gearing and distortions of comparisons with prior years.

Debt Restructuring

Debt is borrowed money from an outside source with commitment to repay the principal plus agreed interest at specified periods. In a turnaround situation, debt restructuring involves renegotiating and reducing monetary obligations to improve or restore liquidity and rehabilitate the company for continued operation. This process often requires rescheduling, refinancing and sale of equity based on negotiations with creditors and other stakeholders. Debt restructuring helps to pay creditors in a timely manner, build company reputation, reduce the likelihood of litigation and improve relationships between the company and key stakeholders such as suppliers. Negotiations with lenders become easier if the struggling firm has a past record of reliability but has recently fallen on hard times.

Rescheduling refers to the practice of extending the terms of an existing loan in order to defer the repayment period. This may involve a delay in the due dates of required payments or reducing payment amounts by extending the payment period and increasing the number of payments. Consolidation refinancing involves replacing existing debt obligations, including outstanding or overdue amounts, with a new instrument under different terms. The lender provides the company with funding to cover existing debts and starts a new debt instrument under different terms such as a lower rate of interest. Managers should read the contracts very carefully and make comparisons between all terms and conditions including interest rates, total finance charges and other fees. In particular, interest rates should not become more punitive over time. Personal guarantees may be required. Before refinancing, managers should verify the integrity and history of the lending institution and evaluate exactly how the refinancing plan works.

Mechanisms for Restructuring

Firms may use court proceedings, private workouts or a hybrid mechanism to resolve financial distress depending on the net benefit of each option. Insolvency regimes allow a market economy to operate more efficiently by providing an enabling environment for company restructuring. Although these court proceedings offer protection against adverse creditor actions, they are usually lengthy, costly and carry stigma that can harm a company's image.

In Jamaica, the Companies Act of 2004 makes provisions for corporate insolvency to wind-up or liquidate the distressed firm. Even unsecured creditors can petition the court to enforce contractual obligations to pay debts. The court may issue an order for seizure and sale of company assets or appoint a receiver. The receiver is required to take custody and control of assets subject to the charge and realize them to satisfy the debt. Generally, the receiver is not authorized to carry on the business of the company. The process of winding-up a company involves its dissolution and removal from the Register of Companies.

The distressed company may be rescued through the court, by either a compromise arrangement or amalgamation and reconstruction. Compromise arrangements pay less than original contractual amounts and are binding on all creditors, whether agreeing or dissenting. Amalgamation and reconstruction occur rarely because court-appointed administrators are not yet part of the insolvency law in Jamaica. Moreover, these court options are unsuitable for small enterprises because of the expense involved, which leaves liquidation as the inevitable outcome for these enterprises.

Interestingly, a new bankruptcy and insolvency act is under review in Jamaica and will introduce provisions for company rehabilitation. The distressed company will be able to file a petition with the court and provide proof of all alleged facts in the document. The court will appoint a supervisor over the assets and operations of the company and grant a stay of proceedings brought against the company by its creditors. Management is given a period of time to submit a turnaround plan and this is discussed with creditors to arrive at a workable way forward for company recovery as a going concern.

Private workouts are preferred for firms that have simple capital structures, substantial intangible assets, and few conflicting positions among claimants or good cash flow potential (Gilson, John & Lang, 1990). Workouts are less costly and faster than other mechanisms for resolving financial distress. Agreements can be reached quickly, assuming the creditor does not hold out, or decides to disagree to the terms, in hopes of getting a better deal. Though a swift process, the private workout mechanism carries the risk of a run on assets by creditors who are often reluctant to negotiate workouts because of the option to trigger receivership.

Shrader and Hickman (1993) stated that two important decision variables include the value of a firm and the net benefits of alternative methods for restructuring. Chatterjee, Dhillon, and Ramirez (1996) observed that firms adopting workouts had higher operating cash flows than those resorting to bankruptcy reorganization. These researchers also found that firms having recalcitrant creditors and substantial bank debt filed for bankruptcy protection. Asquith, Gertner, and Scharfstein (1990) argued that banks were reluctant to provide debt relief because their exposure is secured. Furthermore, pre-packaged bankruptcy is used by firms that have strong cash flow potential but face immediate liquidity problems (Chatterjee, et al., 1996).

Logically, managers of a distressed firm should opt for private workout because this mechanism is less costly, faster and avoids the stigma of bankruptcy. However, when managers perceive a threat of a run-on assets by creditors, bankruptcy reorganization will be chosen as a pre-emptive move to maximize firm protection (Moulton & Thomas, 1993). In pursuing a workout, if management encounters a hold-out problem, then pre-packaged bankruptcy reorganization will be attempted. If the workout fails outright, managers will petition the court for blanket bankruptcy protection. Irrespective of mechanism, the end result is either firm rehabilitation or liquidation.

Figure 3.1 shows how to navigate the process for resolving financial distress with explicit recognition of the major mechanisms for resolving financial distress. A firm is viable if the net present value of its cash flows exceeds the value of net assets. Turnaround plans need to demonstrate that the new debt arrangements are affordable even when the assumptions are conservative.

Bankruptcy Reorganization

Legislation for bankruptcy reorganization is forthcoming in Jamaica to enable company rehabilitation by way of a court-supervised process of breaking and rewriting financial contracts. This mechanism aims to settle claims against the indebted firm in an orderly fashion, and the court provides a legal channel for resolving conflicts. Bankruptcy reorganization seeks to rehabilitate the distressed firm while protecting the interests of creditors (Moulton & Thomas, 1993). However, these proceedings can vary in terms of management and control rights (Hashi, 1997). In the United States and Germany, incumbent management is responsible for submitting and implementing the plan for

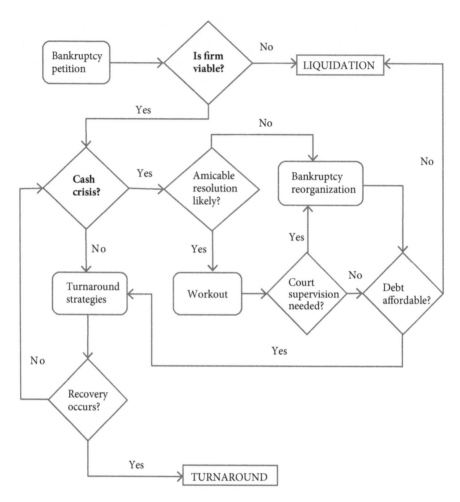

Figure 3.1. How to resolve financial distress

reorganization. However, in Germany, the court gives management far less discretionary powers in executing the plan. In France and the United Kingdom, incumbent management is replaced by a receiver. This individual is appointed by creditors and the court in the United Kingdom and France, respectively. The receiver is responsible for preparing and administering the plan for company rehabilitation.

In the United States, a firm is protected by an automatic stay of claims, but it might have certain operational restrictions such as a threshold debt to assets ratio. This is aimed at averting unjustified risk taking by management. In France, the plan for reorganization is also binding on a firm and its creditors. However, in the United Kingdom, the receiver can decide to wind down the firm even if its going concern value exceeds liquidation value. In Germany, although firms must pay all creditors a stipulated percentage of their claims in cash, creditors can still opt to liquidate their security to recoup outstanding amounts.

Cost, time and stigma are the major disadvantages of bankruptcy reorganization (Moulton & Thomas, 1993). Direct costs include professional fees, court expenses and other incidentals. These costs can range from 3 per cent of liabilities for large companies to over 20 per cent for small firms (Weiss, 1990; White, 1983). Indirect costs include loss of bargaining power and difficulty in establishing long-term contracts. The proceedings can be lengthy. Some firms take more than three years from filing to completion (Moulton & Thomas, 1993). Furthermore, the stigma of bankruptcy can harm company image and destroy the careers of managers and directors (Gilson, 1989 and 1990).

Private Workouts

The benefits of private workouts arise primarily by avoiding the disadvantages of bankruptcy. Workouts do not carry the expenses associated with formal judicial proceedings. Also, in the absence of court bureaucracy, agreements can be reached in a more timely manner. Moreover, both debtors and creditors are more likely to be satisfied with the outcome of a workout rather than a set of conditions imposed by the court (Finkelstein, 1993).

There are, however, some potential disadvantages to workouts. Firstly, an influential creditor might decide not to agree to the workout in the hope of receiving full payment if other creditors accept the new arrangement. This "holdout" problem can delay the implementation of important changes decided by the workout, which can work to the detriment of the firm and its creditors. One solution to this dilemma is to opt for a pre-packaged bankruptcy reorganization plan (McConnell & Servaes, 1991). In this case, a firm solicits majority creditors' acceptance of a plan for company rehabilitation. Management then files for bankruptcy reorganization. Given the advanced negotiation with creditors, a confirmation hearing can be scheduled quickly leading to an early exit from bankruptcy. This action allows the majority creditors to bind the minority creditors legally but, unfortunately introduces court-related expenses for the filing firm (Hansen & Salerno, 1991).

Another potential disadvantage of private workouts is the perception by creditors that the proposal from management is unreasonable. Here, creditors are likely to reject the plan for rehabilitation believing that a better solution can be obtained. If continued negotiations fail to resolve this problem, a firm is likely to begin formal bankruptcy proceedings or even liquidation. Interestingly, Gilson (1989) observed that the majority of managers who avoided bankruptcy reorganization and opted for workouts lost their jobs within two years of company restructuring.

Sale of Equity

Equity refers to the ownership interest or claim of shareholders in a firm. This is the net worth of the firm defined as funds contributed by owners and adjusted for retained earnings or accumulated losses. In a turnaround situation, equity is often sold by way of either rights issue or a debt/equity swap.

Rights issue refers to an offer of new stocks to existing shareholders in proportion to their current holdings for a specified period and usually at a discounted price. This provides cash for the firm while affording shareholders the opportunity of maintaining their percentage of ownership. Company image, brand and performance history are important factors influencing the success of a rights issue. A firm may also need to increase the authorized share capital in preparation for the rights issue.

A debt/equity swap refers to the exchange of debt for a specified amount of equity. Typically, the value of the swap is done at market rates, but a distressed firm may need to make concessions in order to entice debt holders to participate. After the swap, the preceding asset class (the debt) is cancelled in favour of the newly acquired asset class (the equity).

Leveraging Public Relations

Public relations (PR) refer to communications directed primarily toward enhancing credibility with the entities that the debtor needs to remain in business. This is an important part of the turnaround plan and involves clear and honest messages to help create organizational stability as well as combat fear and ignorance. Public opinion can easily become the belief of key stakeholders. A good PR programme helps to buy time for turnaround to take place. This involves deciding the core messages, who will speak on behalf of the company, the timing and manner of communications and how feedback will be handled.

Outcomes

Bankruptcy reorganization and workouts are the primary channels used to reduce company debt burden to an affordable level (Lawrence & Jones, 2001). However, turnaround managers face a trade-off between the need to expedite company rehabilitation and the need to protect the firm against adverse creditor actions. There is no dominant perspective about the likelihood of resolving financial distress.

Some firms undergoing bankruptcy reorganization continue to have weak debt ratios and are likely to require further debt restructuring. Yet, the company's performance can be acceptable in the period following reorganization (Alderson & Betker, 1999; Jog, Kotlyar, & Tate, 1993). Moreover, there is no great disparity between firms opting for workouts and those going the route of bankruptcy reorganization. For example, Gilson, John, and Lang (1990) noted that 47 per cent of affected firms resolved distress through workouts while 51 per cent opted for bankruptcy reorganization. However, studies show that there is a growing preference for pre-packaged bankruptcy reorganization (Bekter, 1995; McConnell & Servaes, 1991; Hansen & Salerno, 1991).

Small Business Restructuring

Small- and medium-sized enterprise (SME) refers to an independently owned commercial small- or medium-sized business that has subscribed equity capital not exceeding J$500 million (Jamaica Stock Exchange, 2011). SMEs are important for economic growth and job creation. However, they have a relatively high rate of discontinuance. There is scant literature about how SMEs act to reverse losses and financial distress. This issue needs urgent attention by researchers because SMEs have limited resources and revenue streams (Welsh & White, 1981). A wrong response to declining performance wastes already scarce resources and thus hastens the SME's demise.

SME bankruptcy usually occurs due to a lack of business management skills, financial problems and harsh economic climates (Carter & Van Auken, 2006).

Contextual factors such as decline severity, firm productivity and resource availability determine probability of turnaround (Francis & Desai, 2005). Financial losses and inability to obtain affordable financing are primary reasons for SME failure and low growth.

Firms can use financial restructuring to increase liquidity and reduce the cost of capital (Bowman & Singh, 1993). This process involves changes in asset composition, capital structure or terms of debt repayment. Yet, the information available on financial restructuring of large corporations far outweighs similar research on SMEs (Salazar, Soto & Mosqueda, 2012). Using the ABI Inform/ Global electronic database, the author conducted a keyword search of "corporate financial restructuring", which returned 22,793 scholarly journal articles on large corporations; a similar search on SME financial restructuring yielded only 1,115 (or 5 per cent) results.

Welsh and White (1981) noted that resource poverty and limited revenue streams make smaller companies more vulnerable to environmental jolts. Furthermore, SMEs have different financing patterns from large firms (Welsh & White, 1981). Understanding viable financing patterns is important for SME turnaround or growth (Beck, Demirguc-Kunt & Maksimovic, 2008).

SMEs often lack the financial information needed to make successful decisions. Also, firms in a small open economy, such as Jamaica, must cope with the adverse effects of macroeconomic challenges of high interest rates, local currency depreciation and tight liquidity. Academic studies support a positive association between financial strategies and SME performance. For example, debt restructuring can facilitate recovery of distressed SMEs from declining performance (Silva & Santos, 2012). Furthermore, low debt acquisition and effective liquidity management are among the factors promoting profitability and growth of SMEs (Laitinen, 2011). However, no systematic evidence exists about which financial restructuring strategies to choose that will fit different SME business situations. Small business decision-making is often intuitive, informal and invisible (Burvic & Bartlett, 2003). SME owners/managers often strongly influence decision-making in their firms, including whether or not strategies for financial restructuring are adopted. For example, since 2009, the Government of Jamaica has provided substantial tax incentives for SMEs to list on the Jamaica Stock Exchange. After five years, most owner/managaers have shunned the incentive and only nineteen SMEs have taken up this opportunity.

The experience of Salada Foods, a Jamaican producer of instant coffee, illustrates how financial restructuring can be part of a SME's turnaround from losses and insolvency (figure 3.2). This company suffered from the adverse effects of

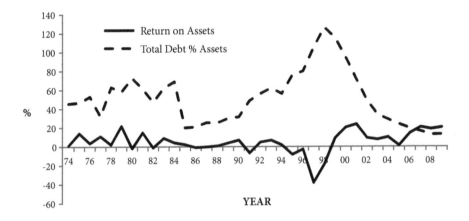

Figure 3.2. Salada Foods leveraged financial restructuring for business turnaround
Source: Jamaica Stock Exchange yearbooks.

hyperinflation and a failed project overseas. To stem decline, management rescheduled debt, sold the loss-making project and negotiated with creditors to refinance debt at a lower rate of interest. Salada Foods also used proceeds from a rights issue of ordinary shares to finance sales growth during its recovery phase of the turnaround cycle.

The appropriate financial strategy for the SME depends on its performance objective and business strategy. Firms engaged in contraction or cutback may wish to sell assets in order to finance a refocusing on core competitive strengths. In contrast, firms in pursuit of growth or expansion may sell equity and defer debt repayment through rescheduling or refinancing to boost liquidity (Silva & Santos, 2012).

To glean insights about how Jamaican SMEs choose from among these financial strategies, 127 owners/managers were interviewed using a pre-tested survey questionnaire (Lawrence, 2013). This sample represented just over 1 per cent of small firms filing General Consumption Tax returns in Jamaica. The data was split into two sub-groups based on the perceived importance of rising debt: The Turnaround group (scoring rising debt at either 4 or 5 on the five point numeric scale) and the Growth group (scoring rising debt at 1, 2 or 3 on the scale).

SME owners/managers in the Turnaround group perceived that debt rescheduling and debt refinancing were of moderate importance while the sale of assets and equity were viewed as of low importance (table 3.2). However, all four strategies for financial restructuring were of low importance for the Growth group (table 3.3).

Table 3.2. Descriptive Statistics and Correlation Coefficients for SME Turnaround

	Mean	s.d.	1	2	3	4	5	6	7	8
1 NewMkt	3.67	1.36								
2 NewProd	3.78	1.34	.19							
3 CutProd	2.15	1.89	.19	.07						
4 ReschedDebt	3.33	1.43	.18	.35**	-.11					
5 SellAssets	1.87	1.21	.01	.18	.31**	.25*				
6 SellEquity	1.76	0.97	.26*	.13	.27*	.23	.63**			
7 Refinance	3.20	1.55	.08	.28**	.14	.48**	.41**	.34**		
8 Age	3.23	1.53	-.23*	-.00**	-.30**	.08	-.05	-.29**	-.24	
9 Employees	2.33	1.06	-.12	-.16	-.03	-.36**	.01	-.12	.33**	.48**

* $p < .10$, ** $p < .05$, two-tailed Spearman tests, N = 54, s.d. is standard deviation

Table 3.3. Descriptive Statistics and Correlation Coefficients for SME Growth

	Mean	s.d.	1	2	3	4	5	6	7	8
1 NewMkt	3.41	1.41								
2 NewProd	3.25	1.30	.61**							
3 CutProd	1.67	0.99	.02	-.06						
4 ReschedDebt	2.37	1.27	.23*	.11	.32**					
5 SellAssets	1.55	1.00	.11	.05	.29**	.08				
6 SellEquity	1.62	1.04	.12	.02	.40**	.20	.65**			
7 Refinance	2.01	1.31	.02	.06	.28**	.46**	.16	.33**		
8 Age	2.89	1.53	-.03	-.14	-.14	-.33**	-.18	-.30**	-.13	
9 Employees	1.82	0.89	.10	-.09	.30**	-.00	.16	.23*	.26**	.22*

* $p < .10$, ** $p < .05$, two-tailed Spearman tests, N = 73, s.d. refers to standard deviation

There was a significant difference between the Turnaround and Growth groups in respect to the addition of new products (Mann Whitney U = 1473.0, p = .012), product cutback (U = 1523.0, p = .017), debt rescheduling (U = 1114.5, p = .000), sale of assets (U = 1680.0, p = .099) and debt refinancing (U = 1115.0, p = .000). SME owners/managers of firms in the Turnaround group placed more emphasis on strategies for debt rescheduling, sale of assets and debt refinancing than SME owners/managers of firms in the Growth group.

In the Turnaround group, for SMEs following a business strategy of contraction, the required strategies for financial restructuring are debt rescheduling, sale of assets and sale of equity (figure 3.3). SMEs attempting turnaround by way of expansion need to refinance debt and sell equity. SMEs in pursuit of revenue

SME Strategy

		Contraction	Expansion
SME Performance Objective	**Turnaround**	A Sell assets Sell equity	B Reschedule debt Sell equity Refinance debt
	Growth	C Reschedule debt Sell assets Sell equity Refinance debt	D Reschedule debt

Figure 3.3. A framework for deciding SME strategies for financial restructuring

growth by way of cutbacks should adopt all four strategies for financial restructuring. SMEs using expansion strategies for revenue growth should reschedule debt.

SME owners/managers perceive that the sale of assets and the sale of equity are appropriate strategies for firms attempting turnaround by way of contraction (Quadrant A in figure 3.3). These actions can solve debt repayment problems even under conditions of impending insolvency. Firms in Quadrant B should reschedule debt, sell equity and refinance debt. These actions help SMEs to boost cash flow for sales growth. SMEs in Quadrant C require all four strategies to refocus on core strengths and build competitive advantage. Firms in Quadrant D are in good financial health and only need breathing space, by way of debt rescheduling, to expand for sales growth.

4 | Changing Strategy and Structure

When organizational decline stems from external forces, a firm requires a new strategy to regain harmony with its environment (Schendel, Patton & Riggs, 1976). Delaying strategy adjustment hastens business failure. For example, when Jamaica Citizens Bank embarked on a programme of rapid expansion from the late 1980s to mid-1990s, the bank increased its number of branches from nine to sixteen and experienced robust revenue growth. However, during this expansion, the local economy slipped into recession with rising interest rates and substantial depreciation of the Jamaican dollar. By 1997, Jamaica Citizens Bank began to report losses and ultimately merged with other financial institutions after an intervention by the government to rescue the troubled financial services sector.

In rapidly changing environments, firms need dynamic capabilities to quickly develop a new competitive advantage by reconfiguring competences and deploying resources for business renewal (Teece, Pisano & Shuen, 1997). Strategy changes occur at three levels. At the corporate level, the aim is to expand, contract or restructure a firm's business portfolio. Business-level strategy looks at how a firm competes in each industry. Typically, this is done by competing on cost leadership, to offer lower prices, or product differentiation to provide superior non-price benefits (Porter, 2008). At the functional level, a firm needs to have adequate customer demand and cost-efficient supply systems that are supported by sufficient financial resources in line with its propensity for taking risks.

Competition often triggers strategic change. When more competitors entered the beverage industry in the aftermath of the 1991 trade liberalization, Desnoes and Geddes divested several business lines to refocus on brewed products. Palace Amusement Company reacted to the growing popularity of cable television by closing several cinemas across the island and reconfiguring the rest to offer customers a choice of the latest movies at each theatre. Faced with an increasing number of local radio stations, Radio Jamaica acquired the television station of the Jamaica Broadcasting Corporation to diversify its stream of revenues.

Other external reasons for changing business strategy include onerous input prices, product maturation, economic recession and natural disasters. Jamaica Producers Group, a diversified and vertically integrated company in agribusiness, decided to exit its UK-based operations that supplied premium organic foods and desserts because of a 32 per cent increase in raw material commodity prices in an economic recession year. The company also ceased banana cultivation in and exports from Jamaica after Hurricane Gustav destroyed its crop. Company revenues fell subsequently by over 50 per cent with steep losses for two consecutive years (figure 4.1). Jamaica Producers Group achieved turnaround by focusing on fruit juices, snacks and freight services in the Caribbean region.

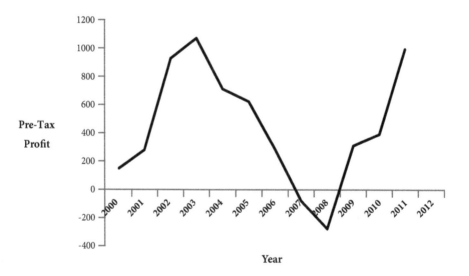

Figure 4.1. Profit recovery at Jamaica Producers Group based on strategic change
Source: Jamaica Stock Exchange yearbooks.

Choosing Turnaround Strategy

When faced with external pressures, such as economic recession or product maturation, business portfolio cutback may reduce the level of investment exposure to fit available demand. Expansion is the optimal strategy if there is unmet demand for which a firm has a competitive advantage. If the reason for decline is low competitiveness or inefficiency, a firm may restructure through cutbacks in some areas and expansion in others. Table 4.1 shows some typical corporate and business level strategies for company turnaround.

Diversification, a corporate turnaround strategy, introduces new businesses that may be related (concentric) or unrelated (conglomerate) to a firm's current portfolio. When expanding internationally, a firm may either adopt a global posture, in which standardized products are sold using the same approach in each market, or a multi-domestic posture, where products and marketing strategies are customized to suit each target country. A firm may also integrate vertically by selling its own outputs (forward integration) to offer customers unique value, or produce its own inputs (backward integration) to lower costs. A troubled firm may invite acquisition by another entity for inclusion in its portfolio based on synergies. For example, Capital and Credit Merchant Bank was affected by falling interest rates and welcomed its acquisition by securities dealer Jamaica Money Market Brokers.

Retrenchment as a corporate strategy refers to a deliberate cutback in a firm's business portfolio to refocus on core strengths and enhance cash flow and efficiency, thereby boosting financial health. Seprod Company, a producer of soaps

Table 4.1. Corporate and business strategies for business renewal

Strategy	Level	Objective
Diversification	Corporate	Multiple revenue streams
International expansion	Corporate	Enter new markets
Vertical integration	Corporate	Supply chain control
Merger/acquisition	Corporate	More market power
Retrenchment	Corporate	Better financial health
Product differentiation	Business	Superior customer benefits
Cost leadership	Business	Lower product prices

and edible oil products, sold its lucrative soap business in the early 1990s to get cash for investment in high-yield Government of Jamaica securities. This bold move substantially enhanced the company's balance sheet strength and liquidity.

At the business level of turnaround strategy, product differentiation is uniquely positioned to attract customers (Porter, 2008). Knowing consumer preference by conducting careful market surveys enables successful differentiation. This strategy is a challenge for most firms listed on the Jamaica Stock Exchange because of the commodity nature of goods and services offered. Successful differentiation occurs when a firm offers desired value that is not only unique in the marketplace but also costly for competitors to imitate. Desnoes and Geddes leveraged the distinctive taste of Red Stripe beer to withstand competition from other brands in the domestic market. Consumers maintained their preference for Red Stripe, and this enabled the firm to make more money.

Another business-level strategy, called cost leadership, involves superior business processes that eliminate waste and operate at high efficiency relative to competitors (Porter, 2008). This strategy seeks to maximize market share. Most firms on the Jamaica Stock Exchange rely heavily on the local market for revenues. However, the small size of this market often induces price wars leading to an untenable race to the bottom for some industry players. Desnoes and Geddes skilfully avoided this adverse situation by leveraging the marketing prowess and networks of its parent company, Diageo, to penetrate export markets.

Balanced Scorecard

After deciding on strategic objectives, managers should use a balanced scorecard to identify strategy implementation initiatives that are specific, measurable, attainable, relevant and timely. The balanced scorecard is a performance management system that helps to align business activities to firm strategy, improve communications and monitor performance (Kaplan & Norton, 1992). A set of strategic objectives, key performance indicators and strategic initiatives are chosen to answer the following questions: How should the organization appear to shareholders? How should the organization appear to customers? What business processes must the organization excel at in order to satisfy its shareholders and customers? How will the organization strengthen and sustain its ability to change and improve?

Strategic objectives focus on the priorities for business renewal and should be derived from a detailed analysis of a firm's strengths, weaknesses, opportunities and threats. The balanced scorecard shows how these objectives relate to each other as a set of cause and effect relationships for turning resources into accomplishments. Each strategic objective has at least one quantifiable measure, called a key performance indicator (KPI), for assessing the extent to which desired outcomes are achieved. A KPI can be either a lag or leading measure and guide development of strategic initiatives, programmes or projects for business renewal. Figure 4.2 shows the balanced scorecard, with a strategy map and key

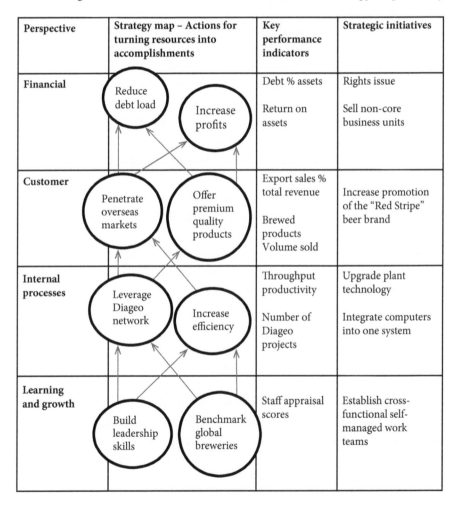

Perspective	Strategy map – Actions for turning resources into accomplishments	Key performance indicators	Strategic initiatives
Financial	Reduce debt load / Increase profits	Debt % assets Return on assets	Rights issue Sell non-core business units
Customer	Penetrate overseas markets / Offer premium quality products	Export sales % total revenue Brewed products Volume sold	Increase promotion of the "Red Stripe" beer brand
Internal processes	Leverage Diageo network / Increase efficiency	Throughput productivity Number of Diageo projects	Upgrade plant technology Integrate computers into one system
Learning and growth	Build leadership skills / Benchmark global breweries	Staff appraisal scores	Establish cross-functional self-managed work teams

Figure 4.2. Desnoes and Geddes' balanced scorecard for business renewal
Source: Company annual reports.

performance indicators for business renewal at Desnoes and Geddes from 1996 to 2001.

The steps for developing an effective balanced scorecard performance management system, with a plan for risk management, are as follows:

1. Review past events and the current situation.
2. Decide what the company wants to become, bearing in mind its values.
3. Decide what the company wants to do and achieve.
4. Identify the major external forces in both the general and industry environments.
5. Identify the major issues pertaining to the internal environment.
6. Make a list of company strengths, weaknesses, opportunities and threats
7. Determine the strategic objectives or priorities for the planning horizon; these objectives should cover finance, customer, internal processes and learning and growth.
8. Develop a balanced scorecard strategy map that links the strategic objectives as a set of cause and effect relationships.
9. Agree on lagging and leading key performance indicators (KPIs) for each strategic objective.
10. Set quarterly targets aligned to each KPI.
11. Determine strategic initiatives (programmes or projects) to achieve the targets.
12. Develop action plans to execute the programmes or projects.
13. Identify the upside (opportunity) and downside (hazard) risks associated with the programmes or projects.
14. Assess the likelihood of occurrence and impact of risks associated with the programmes or projects.
15. Decide company contingency response for each risk.
16. Prepare a plan for communications with stakeholders.

There must be congruence not only across different levels of company strategy but also between strategies and tactics or initiatives. The balanced scorecard helps to convert strategic objectives into specific, measurable, attainable realistic and timely (SMART) projects or routine activities for effective and efficient execution (Kaplan & Norton, 1992). In a turnaround situation, this tool helps management to focus on using scarce resources for strategic initiatives that are most critical for recovery from decline.

Implementing Turnaround Strategy

Strategy implementation is the process of putting selected critical programmes, projects or other activities into action by way of an appropriate organizational structure, people, systems, programmes, budgets and procedures. Managers must not only craft a business renewal strategy but also plan the execution and become deeply engaged in its success (Bossidy & Charan, 2002). The focus should be on a few clear priorities that everyone can grasp. Who will do what and when? Strategic initiatives must be broken down into smaller tasks that can be executed in the short term. Even one non-performer at an influential level in the organization can destroy turnaround efforts and, consequently, the organization. Thus, effective turnaround managers must be decisive on tough issues, able to get things done through others and be able to follow through on commitments. Key questions to be answered during a review of strategy include: How much does each business unit know about the competitors, and what are their likely responses to your strategy? Does the firm have the capability and resources to execute the strategy? Are the key assumptions about the business environment sound?

Time, quality and costs are crucial factors in a turnaround situation. For success, the chosen turnaround strategy must not only be compelling but also driven by a coalition of influential stakeholders. Managerial cognitions can filter important signals from the external environment thereby impeding the actions necessary for recovery from decline. Organizational politics must be managed to build the required support for business renewal.

Strategy execution tends to take longer when projects are implemented sequentially and the change is radical. Best results often arise from linking strategic initiatives to the core values and reward systems of the organization. Quantitative measures or metrics should be used to assess and drive execution, but they must be easy to understand and transparent for maximum effectiveness. Strategies can fail because of resistance to change. This resistance may arise from disagreement on the nature of the organization's problem, the chosen solutions or perceived adverse consequences to those solutions. Managers need to develop the right model for execution, choose appropriate metrics, assess performance frequently and communicate proactively to all levels in the organization to limit resistance. There must be clear responsibility and accountability with a full understanding of who does what, when, why, where and how.

Establishing a culture of discipline and ownership can be challenging in a turnaround situation. To that end, managers should practice forthright, transformational leadership. As far as possible, management decisions and actions must be based on credible information and evidence. Furthermore, tackling too many priority decisions simultaneously can overwhelm even the strongest management teams. Priorities should be set in logical order by honestly appraising the team's existing capabilities for turnaround strategy execution.

Firms need to explore ways to avoid unnecessary competition by finding ways to collaborate through partnerships and other forms of alliances. Managers should build accountability into meetings and set milestones linked directly to the turnaround plan. Firms should also encourage candid dialogue and confront performance issues to uncover workable solutions.

Business renewal does not occur automatically. The collective members of a firm need to apply five fundamental disciplines for acquiring and using knowledge and insights (Senge, 1990). "Systems thinking" is a conscious effort to see the big picture beyond the clutter of details. Personal mastery involves directing energies toward important goals by continually clarifying the vision and developing the competences needed for success. Mental models challenge assumptions about how the world works and rethink traditional paths to success with openness to new paradigms. Building a shared vision develops commitment to a common picture of the future. Team learning involves thinking together to discover insights based on collective reasoning.

Organizational culture refers to the psychology, attitudes, experiences, beliefs and values emanating from the totality of people, systems and structures in place to implement strategies and tactics. To create the correct culture for business renewal, Desnoes and Geddes prioritized its strategic initiatives based on expected impact, resources required and time for completion. The parent company, Diageo, set standards to guide performance within and across departments. Desnoes and Geddes used media releases to generate excitement about its projects, even plant upgrading. Management had open lines of communication. Cross-functional teams were formed to expedite projects. Pay incentives were used to reinforce change.

Organizational Structure

Firms also need to have an appropriate organizational structure for implementing a business renewal strategy. The organizational structure is a formal system of tasks and reporting relationships that coordinates and motivates employees to work together. Although hybrid organizational structures are sometimes used, managers tend to choose one of four basic types of organizational structures depending on the scope of products and markets (figure 4.3).

A purely functional structure is required if the scope of products and market are both narrow. Functional structures consist of departments or people grouped together based on similar skills or knowledge to perform jobs such as marketing, operations, finance and accounting, and human resources. Each department might include additional subgroups. For example, marketing departments can have advertising, sales and research teams. The functional structure works best when the organization has well-developed products in a relatively stable market.

A product structure is required when the scope of goods or services is wide and the scope of market is narrow. Each division of the organization specializes in only one product area thereby building expertise for differentiation or cost leadership. The product structure puts divisional managers close to their customers for quick response in changing industry environments.

A market or geographic structure is suitable when the organization has a narrow scope of products but wide scope of market. Managers are given full responsibility for the operations and performance of a specific territory. This arrangement helps a firm best respond to the unique demands of particular geographic areas or customers.

A matrix structure should be used when the organization has a wide scope of products and also wide scope of market. This simultaneously groups people and resources by function and product. Each person in a matrix team reports to two supervisors: a product manager and a geographic region manager. This arrangement brings special expertise to the unique needs of various customers but tends to have higher overhead costs.

A flat organizational structure, having no more than three levels of management, affords a better responsiveness to environmental changes. Decentralization of authority is a way to keep the organization flat. This works best

MARKET SCOPE

		NARROW	WIDE
PRODUCT SCOPE	NARROW	FUNCTIONAL	MARKET
	WIDE	PRODUCT	MATRIX

Figure 4.3. Choose organizational structure for business renewal

using well-understood technology with staple products such as certain foods or accounting services. Downsizing is one way to strip away excess jobs and staff but managers must be mindful of improving employee morale, quality and efficiency.

Small Business Strategies

SMEs tend to create more jobs as they become older, but they are also more likely to fail because of high input prices, inefficient operations and low market penetration (Lawrence, 2007/8). Cutback in waste and expenditure and tighter internal controls are common small business responses for recovery from performance decline (Snyder, 1999; Hofer, 1980). These actions can involve downsizing the workforce:

- reducing inventory
- implementing cutbacks in selling and administration expenditures
- decreasing the cost of goods sold
- collecting accounts receivable
- increasing prices
- stretching accounts payable

While these cutback options often prove useful for SMEs, some turnarounds take place without resorting to cutbacks (Arogyaswamy & Yasai-Ardekani, 1997) by increasing the money generated from sales, called "throughput" (Bushong & Talbott, 1999). According to the Theory of Constraints, the key to maximizing profit is to produce and sell goods and services that provide the most throughput per unit of the constraining factor (Goldratt, 1997). Every productive system has a constraint that inhibits the ability of a firm to make money now and in the future. This bottleneck can be internal, such as the inability to fulfil customer orders, or external, as in weak demand. When the constraint is inside the company, managers should begin by setting the pace of the entire productive system at the speed of the constraint. This technique ensures that the bottleneck operates at its capacity with no idle time or rework. Then, by co-opting resources from non-bottleneck areas or making additional investment to expand capacity, management can explore ways to increase throughput at this constraint. Once a constraint is broken, a new bottleneck arises and the approach is repeated in a process of ongoing improvement.

5 | Increasing Operations Efficiency

The roadmap for business renewal shows that, irrespective of the turnaround situation, a firm needs to increase its operations efficiency by generating more output of goods and services while consuming less of resource inputs. Companies are challenged to generate profitable demand and keep abreast with supply without compromising quality or cost. There are several ways to increase efficiency, including increasing the scale or scope of products and market output, reducing waste, improving the supply chain and using appropriate technologies more effectively.

While a firm may expand its output when sufficient resources are available, it must cut back if there is a deficiency. Cash rich Courts Jamaica expanded the scope and scale of output by broadening its range of products with new items, such as personal computers and gym equipment, and increased its reach by adding more branches to its network of retail stores. Courts Jamaica also installed a new computerized system for managing inventory. The Gleaner Company possessed the resources to introduce new technology for circulating newspapers. However, Salada Foods had severe resource constraints and therefore was forced not only to reduce costs through staff cutbacks and shedding its marketing department, but also to adjust its supply chain by terminating its sole distributor, and contracting the services of three other companies instead.

Even with very limited financial resources, a firm can enhance its customer service, the process of satisfying the users of a product, to boost revenues. Critical success factors for effective customer service include increased employee morale and commitment. Managers should provide clear communications about the level of customer service expected from employees and provide commensurate incentives, staff development and leadership informed by relevant research about consumer profiles and behaviour. Effective customer service often generates revenues through increased customer loyalty and referrals.

In a turnaround situation, efficient cost cutting can stop cash haemorrhage and reduce the amount of revenues required for company break-even. Companies may consider business process re-engineering to eliminate waste and improve specifications. Other approaches include substitution without compromising quality, outsourcing non-critical functions, automation and new technologies, variable employee compensation, and flexible workforce size. Managers should evaluate the potential effectiveness of options for cutting costs based on criteria such as impact and timeliness.

Desnoes and Geddes

Desnoes and Geddes entered the decade of the 1990s as the market leader with a wide range of beverages including beer, stout, carbonated drinks, rums, wines and spirits. However, by 1993, the company's performance started to decline because of price competition. By 1995, the company reported an 11 per cent decline in sales and a 3 per cent loss margin, plus a working capital deficit. This was coupled with a strike by unionized workers who had shut down production at both of its plants.

To this point, Desnoes and Geddes competed on the bases of quality and flexibility using a wide range of reputable local beverage brands including Red Stripe and Dragon Stout as well as global brands under licence such as Pepsi-Cola, Heineken, Schweppes and Guinness. The company responded to price competition by changing its mix of priorities to quality, delivery and cost. Desnoes and Geddes downsized its workforce by over 40 per cent and divested shares in a bottle-making and lithographic printing company. Production was consolidated under one plant, and technology was upgraded in the soft drink lines and plastic bottle packaging. Faced with intensifying competition, in 1999, the company withdrew from the production of carbonated beverages, wines and spirits to focus on beers and stouts only (see table 5.1).

Desnoes and Geddes installed new equipment for more automation of its processes and expanded its brewing capacity. The company also invested

Table 5.1. Priorities, Products and Performance at Desnoes and Geddes

	Period of Decline 1992–1995	Decline-Stemming 1995–1998	Recovery 1998–2001
Priorities	Quality Flexibility	Quality Flexibility Cost	Quality Delivery Cost
Products	Beer, stouts, carbonated drinks, wines, spirits	Beer, stouts, carbonated drinks, wines, spirits	Beer, stouts
Avg Return on Assets	7.3%	-0.1%	28.2%

heavily in promoting Red Stripe as a premium quality beer. Production volumes increased and the level of exports climbed to 20 per cent of total output. Waste reduction became a major driver of efficiency improvements. Desnoes and Geddes embraced the five disciplines of organizational learning put forward by Senge (1990):

- systems thinking to see the big picture,
- personal mastery to develop the required competences and direct energy toward important goals,
- mental models to challenge assumptions about the path to success,
- building a shared vision for collective commitment to a common picture of the future, and
- team learning to discover new insights from collective reasoning.

Rather than employing a bureaucratic, top-down approach, Desnoes and Geddes coached cross-functional, self-managed work teams to solve productivity problems.

The company was intent on offering world-class brands at globally competitive prices by focusing on total quality management (TQM) as a means to exceed customer expectations, integrate systems for seamless physical connectivity, enhance real time information flow, and use lean practices for enhanced product delivery at minimum cost. Customers were treated as business partners with whom the firm made frequent consultations. Big breweries in the United States, Brazil and Venezuela were benchmarked to identify projects for continuous improvement. The financial, logistical, manufacturing and human resource computer databases were integrated into one system for better data access, transfer and communication. All processes were reviewed in respect of value-added, time, duration and consistency in order to squeeze unnecessary costs out of company systems.

Some important insights arose from turnaround at Desnoes and Geddes:

1. The best way to increase efficiency depends on the firm-specific context.
2. Projects can be used to fast-track efficiency gains.
3. The extent of the increase in efficiency depends upon the proper alignment of the competitive priorities established by the firm and its operational activities.

Systems Analysis

Everything in operations management involves systems. However, what works for one firm can be inappropriate for another. Managers should carefully apply the principles of General Systems Theory as follows:

1. Identify the critical decision variables for the specific context at hand.
2. Collect and analyse data relevant to the critical variables.
3. Develop a workable action plan to adjust the critical variables in line with the outcomes of the systems analysis.

Context-specific critical decision variables can be identified by mapping specific operations in terms of input resources, how value is added, output of goods and services and the way controls are maintained. Typically, input resources include technology, people, materials and capital. Value is determined based on a firm's layout, production capacity, business processes that are utilized and whether the facility is located in an appropriate area. Outputs are described in terms of volume generated, product diversity and design of goods and services. Major control variables focus on scheduling, quality, supply chain and maintenance.

When analysing systems toward developing an action plan, choosing the appropriate technology is an important component. Typically, the break-even point of the business increases with more automation. Therefore, managers need to be assured that sufficient market demand exists before automating. A firm should also consider the cost and timing of facilities and equipment maintenance, including its potential level of investment in preventative maintenance.

Another important component of cultivating a workable action plan involves incentivizing employees. The nature of rewards and incentives offered to employees can either promote or derail business renewal efforts. Thus, managers should assess potential productivity gains from individual incentives versus group schemes and review these choices periodically. For example, when company employees perceive routinely paid incentives to be automatic regardless of employee performance, there will be few productivity gains from the rewards plan. This situation may be avoided by adopting incentives that are randomized and awarded based on performance.

Performing routine systems analyses can illuminate important information for creating business renewal strategies. For example, excess capacity of employees can exacerbate profit decline due to embedded costs such as payroll, maintenance and insurance expenses that do not necessarily increase related revenues. However, revenues are lost if employee capacity is insufficient. Capacity planning should take revenue seasonality into account. Management should consider options for temporary increases in capacity such as temporary staffing, before making permanent arrangements.

Company waste is an additional component that systems analyses can discern. Waste can creep into company processes over time. Firms are advised to periodically map work processes and eliminate non-specified activities. Business process reengineering can also reduce costs through changes in specifications and flow. Queues or waiting lines often arise when the rate at which the company is able to deliver services falls short of customers demand. Managers need to consider intangibles, such as reputational risks, when assessing the benefits versus the costs of waiting lines.

Supply Chain Management

When there are pronounced shifts in customer attitudes and behaviours, cost-cutting and asset retrenchment are insufficient strategies for business renewal. In this scenario, supply chain management is a necessary strategic weapon to chart the way forward. Supply chain refers to a flow of activities and transactions (involving information, money, goods and services) from suppliers through producers, distributors and retailers to end users (UNCTAD, 2010).

There can be several tiers of suppliers and customers. Flows of goods or services from supplier to customer are called logistics, and flows in the opposite direction are called reverse logistics. The segment from suppliers towards a firm is called the "upstream" or "inbound" side of the supply chain, while the segment from the firm to customers is called the "downstream" side or "outbound" side of the supply chain. Movement on the inbound side is referred to as "transportation," and movement on the outbound side is called "distribution". Value-added may be goods-oriented, as in the conversion of raw materials into finished products, or service-oriented as in the facilitation or origination of financial transactions. The supply chain may span global networks and often involves the Internet or other electronic media.

Managing supply chains involves planning, organizing, leading and controlling flows of physical and human resources, information, processes, capacity, service performance and funds from the earliest supplier to the ultimate

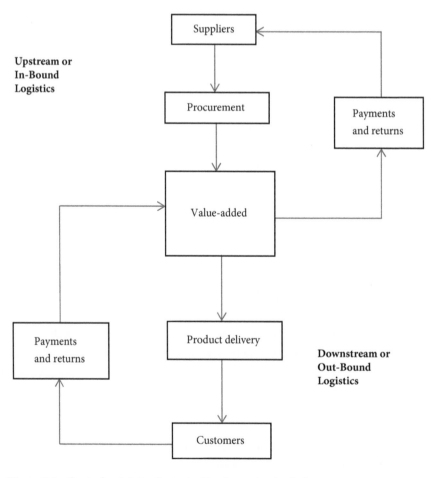

Figure 5.1. Control points in the typical business supply chain

customer. Supply chain management occurs at the functional level of strategy execution and can boost profitability by taking the right products to the right place at the right time and in the right quantities in order to maximize the value and minimize the cost of the product that is delivered to customers.

In the global arena, competition takes place on the basis of supply chains and not merely among individual firms. Moreover, these supply chains change configuration quickly as organizations seek to achieve or sustain their competitive advantage. Financial institutions that fail to assess and adjust supply chains on a timely basis risk declining profitability. Yet, there is scant information on how to adapt service supply chains to changing environments, particularly for service organizations, such as financial institutions, where products are fungible (freely exchangeable in whole or part and in like or kind). Furthermore, supply chains often involve long-term contractual relationships between suppliers, customers and firms. A crucial question arises, then: How should managers choose and leverage supply chains to boost firm profitability? The following discussion provides guidelines for success.

Assessing Supply Chains

On the upstream or inbound logistics side of the supply chain, supplier cooperation and long-term commitment are significant determinants of the extent of financial institutions' satisfaction with supplier performance. On the downstream or outbound logistics side, customer efficiency, in terms of the amount of a firm's resources that are consumed during service delivery, affects business profitability. Moreover, firms need to take a granular account of how all of the supply chain elements fit together, from end to end, to reduce uncertainty and meet the needs of customers in a cost-effective manner. Thus, by assessing and adjusting critical success factors in dynamic ways, firms may align supply chains with a competitive strategy and strengthen transaction flows.

Goods and services are transported to a firm, on the upstream or inbound side of the supply chain, and services are distributed to customers on the downstream or outbound side (figure 5.1). The model shown in figure 5.1 can be scaled to suit supply chain complexity. Key decision areas include choice and number of suppliers, resource procurement, processing of transactions, modes of service delivery and target customers to be served. A firm earns income from operations by creating value for customers based on product appeal, quality, delivery, flexibility and cost.

There may be several tiers of suppliers and customers as well as a portfolio of supply chains within the organization. The supply chain may also span across national borders. Some participants in the supply chain may operate on both the inbound and outbound sides. For example, customers of financial institutions provide deposits or investments while taking loans from the same institution. Firms must also manage reverse logistics involving returns to suppliers or from customers because of errors or changes. For best results, supply chains must be aligned with a competitive strategy and maintain appropriate structures, technical support and control systems that cultivate proper relationships and carry acceptable levels of risk relative to returns.

Strategy

The supply chain is a strategic asset used for executing competitive strategy and achieving a competitive advantage. Typically, a firm has to balance their supply chain strategy through a trade-off between efficiency and responsiveness. Those focused on efficiency tend to offer standard products. Firms geared toward responsiveness often customize products to suit the needs of particular clients.

Firms may also adopt a competitive strategy of cost leadership to pursue economies of scale. This approach is driven by process innovation to reduce costs, maximize efficiency and deliver high output volumes for increased market share and lower prices.

Another strategy, product differentiation, is beneficial when a firm can satisfy unmet customer needs at premium prices. In this situation, the supply chain maximizes profit margins through product innovation that leads to better responsiveness in areas such as service flexibility, customization or customer convenience.

Structure

Supply chain structure and integration are important components for executing competitive strategy. Each business unit and major functional area in a firm needs to create its own supply chain configuration that aligns with the company's mission and strategic objectives while remaining congruent with the rest of the organization.

Managers must also look at the length of the supply chain because risk increases with higher numbers of supplier and customer tiers. Some institutions establish supply chain networks to provide a wider array of products. However, this approach carries reputational risk and higher credit exposure that should be avoided by careful supply chain selection. The extent of participation in the chain, by way of vertical integration or outsourcing, is another factor to be considered. Large institutions tend to be vertically integrated with many inbound services available in-house. Some firms improve customer efficiency by providing outbound services through both physical and virtual channels as well as a choice of either self-service or employee-service formats. Outsourcing can reduce costs, but it also relinquishes control. The supply chain may also be embedded in a cluster of interconnected organizations partnering together for increased productivity and competitiveness.

Systems

Supply chain systems refer to the set of resources, facilities and processes used to generate customer value and benefits for the organization. Capacity and technology are at the heart of these systems.

- *Capacity:* Great care must be taken when establishing the amount of work that a business can handle. Too much capacity elevates the revenues required to break even while too little restricts a firm's earning power. To determine capacity needs, firms must balance demand forecasts over the long-term against short-term variations due to seasonality or other fluctuations. Managers should identify the present constraint to transactions throughput, avoid downtime at the constraint, use other elements in the chain to support the constraint and explore other ways to overcome the constraint until the flow of transactions becomes acceptable.
- *Technology:* Managers should be alert to scientific developments for improving operations and building competitive advantage. Advances in information technology decrease with time and will remove geographical constraints from communications and transactions, while offering more options for service delivery to make supply chains more virtual. Increased computing power and data storage facilitate the use of advanced analytics for faster and more granular decision-making in all

areas including trading and risk management support. Digitization and integrated enterprise-wide systems automate processes for supply chain integration, customer order fulfilment, reports, transparency, compliance and security.

Another common feature is e-commerce, or using technology in a web-based or other environment to facilitate supply chain flows conducted via electronic media such as electronic funds transfer. Transactions conducted over these channels are accompanied by lower per item revenue, which must be matched by lower transaction unit costs achieved by scale efficiencies. Intensified information capabilities, such as customer relationship management systems, are essential for service delivery to meet changing demand and are based both on customer value and the cost of purchasing and employing data mining technologies. Customer relationship management helps institutions to optimize selling and cross-selling of services and also builds customer loyalty using channels such as e-mail or social media tools.

Relationships

A relationship is a connection, association or involvement between parties. Firms may or may not commit financial resources to preserving or improving connections. Normative relationship commitments involve emotional attachment between the parties based on shared goals or values. Instrumental relationship commitments focus on compliance driven by extrinsic rewards or punishment.

Firms must balance supplier, employee, customer and other stakeholder relationships to achieve the required levels of supply chain performance through networking, communications, smart targets and incentives for discretionary effort in support of the firm. Careful supplier selection, based on compatible values, with appropriate partnerships can build cooperation, trust and long-term commitment. Such proactive collaboration across the entire chain allows companies to bring effective and efficient service delivery to end-users.

Another facet of company relationships involves fostering collaborative partnerships among employees. Employees often require training and incentives for creativity and innovation to achieve organizational goals. This includes setting conditions that foster trust – the extent to which a person is confident in, and willing to act on the basis of words, actions and decisions of another – as well as establishing clear parameters for employee discretion – exercise of power to make decisions regarding work focus, resource commitments and time. Firms need first to plan and execute recruiting and retention programmes to have sufficient talented staff, and then to institute career development programmes to retain and retrain existing personnel who best internalize company values. Efforts should be made to translate these initiatives into measurable performance and to deal decisively with under-performers and non-performers. The selection and management of a company's talent pool is a critical determinant of supply chain effectiveness.

Risk

Supply chains are vulnerable to environmental jolts that cause outcomes to vary from expectations. Managers should make risk-adjusted decisions by

1. Identifying and quantifying the likelihood and potential impact of risk factors,
2. Agreeing on the risk appetite of the organization in terms of what is too much or too little,
3. Engaging stakeholders proactively to boost support for the organization,
4. Establishing and disseminating appropriate risk policies, and
5. Executing prudent risk strategies with mitigation plans to cope with sources of risk, and also contingency plans to resolve the consequences of risk.

It is prudent to retain risks that have low probability of occurrence and low supply chain impact. Risks with low probability of occurrence but high impact should be transferred, for example, by way of insurance. Steps should be taken to reduce exposure to risks that have high probability of occurrence and low impact. Risks having high probability of occurrence and high impact should be avoided. Soft issues such as ethics must also be taken into account when assessing risk factors. Risk assumptions need to be conservative with rigorous back-testing and stress testing to determine the efficacy of the risk models used. Managers must also differentiate between businesses that require diversification of risk (e.g. credit) versus businesses that require aggregation of risk (e.g. insurance) as an essential element of value creation.

Strengthening Supply Chains

Critical supply chain factors for boosting profitability include efficiency (cost), responsiveness (timely delivery and flexibility), integration (control), capacity (volume), technology (extent of automation), inventory (input and output), information (timeliness and accuracy), and strength of capital (reserves).

Table 5.2 illustrates how to use a factor rating table to identify opportunities to align and strengthen the supply chain.

1. Score the extent of importance of each of these factors on a scale of 1 to 5,
2. Rank each factor relative to the others based on scores of importance,
3. Assign weights to each factor noting trade-offs such as efficiency versus responsiveness,
4. Assess and quantify the performance status of each factor on a scale of 1 to 10, and
5. Calculate an overall weighted assessment of the strength of the supply chain. This approach facilitates supply chain congruence by aligning the chain with competitive strategy and revealing areas for strengthening.

Supply chain performance should be measured by throughput productivity, defined as the difference between sales and truly variable costs divided by

Table 5.2. Factor Rating Table for Restructuring Supply Chains

	Supply Chain Factor	Weight	1–10 (1 = Weak)	
			Raw Score	Weighted Score
1	Efficiency	0.15	8	1.20
2	Responsiveness	0.05	7	0.35
3	Integration	0.20	6	1.20
4	Capacity	0.10	8	0.80
5	Technology	0.10	4	0.40
6	Inventory	0.10	8	0.80
7	Information	0.10	4	0.40
8	Capital strength	0.20	7	1.40
	Total Score	1.00		6.55

total non-variable operating expenses. Throughput productivity is a metric that links supply chain flows to profitability. Companies need to monitor throughput productivity over time both to detect any need for adjustment and also to benchmark against other organizations. Large firms that have centralized operations, such as information systems, serving several strategic business units simultaneously should compute throughput productivity, for each unit, by allocating shared operating expenses based on the weighted ratio of the unit's direct expenses to sales.

Supply chain management policies should be established with oversight placed in the hands of senior personnel for proactive vigilance on supply chain congruence and value creation. Firms are urged to apply factor rating analysis to align and strengthen supply chains with the results measured on the basis of throughput productivity. This approach is grounded in the following proposition:

$$\text{Firm Profitability} = f(\text{Throughput Productivity})$$
$$= f(\text{Supply Chain Alignment and Strength})$$

Small Business Efficiency

Few small companies undertake the planning needed to align their operations with environmental dictates. These firms often confine operations to tactical roles and do not exploit this function for successful strategic attacks and defences that can overcome disadvantages of size, market share, and even proprietary technology (Hayes & Upton, 1998). Undesirable outcomes are likely when there is a mismatch between the way resources are deployed and the competitive priorities established by a firm. Small firms, in countries like Jamaica, have few strategic options for turnaround. They must rely on operations because they neither have surplus physical assets for retrenchment nor a portfolio of business units for restructuring.

Firms must decide which competitive priorities and resource deployments to adopt for maximum value-added (Lowson, 2005). Based on the principle of equi-finality, embraced by general systems theory, two firms may attempt the same set of competitive priorities, deploy resources in different ways, yet experience similar results.

Operations can also play a strategic role by focusing resources and capabilities on the priorities needed for competitive advantage (Boyer & Lewis, 2002; Adam & Swamidass, 1989). Proper alignment of competitive priorities and resource deployments increases value-added outputs for improved profitability, thereby reducing the likelihood of business closure.

A survey of 101 small business owners/managers in Jamaica revealed that small firms tend to have more employees over time but are also more likely to fail (Lawrence, 2007/8). Product quality is perceived to be the most important competitive priority (table 5.3). However, owners/managers of new businesses are less consistent in their impressions of the significance of this factor. Many owners/managers believed that small firms should compete on the basis of either (1) quality, delivery, and cost or (2) quality and flexibility. Use of labour was viewed as the critical link between resource factors and competitive priorities. Technology was deemed important for using labour and materials. Debt capital was considered the least important resource factor. Business activity (goods versus services), owner/manager gender, firm age, and firm size do not seem to affect these findings.

These research findings agree with Sum, Kow and Chen (2004) that small firms should compete using multiple priorities. However, survey results further imply that small firms should strive most for superior product quality irrespective of the other priorities in the set. Indeed, inconsistent product quality could be a reason for the high rate of small business closures in the early years following start-up.

Table 5.3. Small Business Descriptive Statistics and Correlation Coefficients

	Mean	s.d.	1	2	3	4	5	6	7	8	9
1 **Cost**	3.53	1.25									
2 **Quality**	4.53	0.98	.28**								
3 **Flex**	3.87	1.31	.12	.24*							
4 **Delivery**	4.30	1.11	.26*	.17	.11						
5 **Labour**	4.32	1.06	-.01	.43**	.24*	.37**					
6 **Material**	2.90	1.69	.06	-.09	.03	.02	.08				
7 **Tech**	3.35	1.42	-.17	.02	.20*	.15	.27**	.23*			
8 **Debt**	2.78	1.47	.09	-.07	-.14	-.01	.05	.20*	.15		
9 **Age**	2.25	1.45	-.09	.06	.02	-.14	-.07	.16	-.00	.03	
10 **Size**	1.65	1.11	.08	-.10	.01	.09	.02	.11	.10	.25*	.40**

* $p < .05$, ** $p < .01$, two-tailed tests, N = 101

The findings also imply that, in using the sand-cone sequence, small firms can skip the development of capabilities that are not in the chosen set of competitive priorities. For example, if quality and flexibility make up the set of priorities, the firm should focus firstly on developing quality and then on flexibility because the latter ranks lower on the sand-cone order. Delivery and cost would be omitted because they do not form part of the required set of priorities.

Two sets of competitive priorities have arisen from a survey of managers: (1) quality, delivery and cost or (2) quality and flexibility. Ebben and Johnson (2005) reported evidence showing that small firms that pursued either low cost or flexibility outperformed those attempting to follow both. Therefore, the two sets of competitive priorities both seem worthy of consideration as turnaround strategy because they have no conflict between cost and flexibility. Rather than employee cutbacks, the research findings from the Regression Analysis imply that small firms should use technology to boost labour productivity for turnaround. The owners/managers perceived that use of labour is critical regardless of the set of priorities chosen (table 5.4).

Table 5.4. Results of Simple Regression Analyses

	Model 1 QUAL	Model 2 FLEX	Model 3 DEL	Model 4 LABOR	Model 5 MAT
LABOR	.446**	.359**	.385**		
	(.083)	(.099)	(.082)		
TECH				.255**	.276**
				(.083)	(.108)
Intercept	2.415**	2.244**	2.509**	3.150**	1.702**
	(.341)	(.408)	(.338)	(.289)	(.374)
F-ratio	27.778**	13.016**	21.948**	9.435**	6.488*
R2	.225	.117	.185	.088	.063

Note: Standard errors are shown in parentheses below the coefficients
* $p < .05$, ** $p < .01$, N = 101

6 | Sustaining Profit Recovery

To sustain performance beyond the period of recovery, firms need to have a cushion of resources or surplus, called organizational slack, for discretionary use to mitigate threats and seize opportunities (Cyert & March, 1963). Organizational slack is the difference between total resources and total necessary payments. Slack resources may be available within the company or subject to call, as in reserve borrowing capacity. A typical financial measure of slack is net working capital divided by total sales. Salada Foods received financial help from the Government of Jamaica and, as a result, continued to build slack resources beyond the period of profit recovery (figure 6.1).

At Desnoes and Geddes, organizational slack was 64 per cent, which correlated with its return on assets and increased from a deficit position in 1995 to 16 per cent by 1999. In 2001, the company received a five-year income tax holiday from the Government of Jamaica, which helped to boost slack a further 28 per cent by 2002. However, Desnoes and Geddes had a subsequent relapse with slack slipping to just 8 per cent in 2005 and into deficit again by 2008 (figure 6.2). Management blamed the special consumption tax levied by the Government of Jamaica. However, marketing costs substantially outpaced the company's growth of sales, jumping from 5 per cent to 11 per cent of revenues over the period 2002 to 2010.

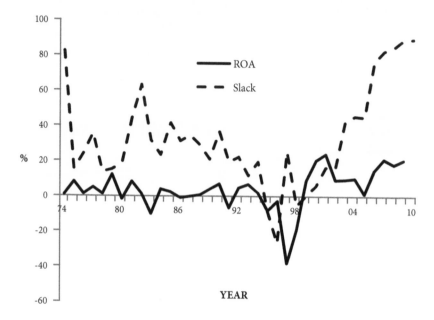

Figure 6.1. Turnaround at Salada Foods
Source: Jamaica Stock Exchange yearbooks.

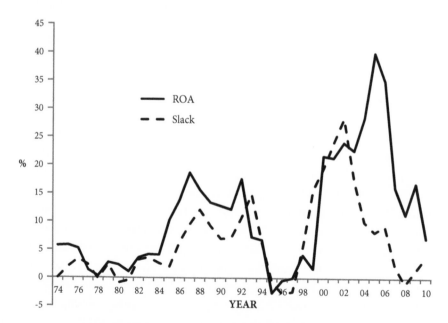

Figure 6.2. Turnaround and relapse at Desnoes and Geddes
Source: Jamaica Stock Exchange yearbooks.

Slack resources influence the amount of risk-taking that companies can pursue as it attempts a turnaround (Singh, 1986). High levels of slack affords more time for recovery in the event that strategic initiatives fail, but too much slack can lead to an underutilization of resources. Companies must often learn from experience how much slack to hold.

Sustainable rate of growth refers to the maximum annual increase in sales that a business can afford without the need to go to external sources for additional support (Higgins, 1977). Firms attempting business renewal need to keep sales within the sustainable rate of growth defined as (ROE multiplied by the retention rate) divided by (1- ROE multiplied by the retention rate), where ROE is return on shareholders' equity, and the retention rate is retained earnings divided by net profit. Managers can use the sustainable rate of growth to check congruence between the firm's growth objective and its financial status.

Strategic Forecasting

To stay ahead of the curve, managers need to anticipate and prepare for future business realities. Forecasting is a popular approach that uses past data and judgement to predict or anticipate future outcomes. The approach recognizes patterns from qualitative assessment data, such as expert opinion, or quantitative analysis using models such as moving average or regression analysis. Figure 6.3 shows that the Gleaner Company may leverage forecasting to inform its strategy for coping with declining newspaper sales. Trends may point to

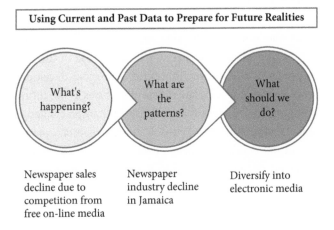

Figure 6.3. A model of strategic forecasting at Gleaner Company

product diversification, or some other turnaround strategy, as the way forward. Irrespective of the approach adopted, potential errors and biases of the forecast should also be taken into account.

Data analytics can enhance business intelligence by profiling persons or phenomena and predicting behaviour in order to spot warning signals and avert organizational decline. Business intelligence enables firms to make strategic, fact-based decisions by

- aggregating large volumes of data,
- reporting data in visual or other formats,
- adding context to enrich the data through descriptive statistics, benchmarking, variance analysis or other applications, and
- transforming data to information by looking at trends, frequencies, sequences, clusters, associations or causation.

Traditional analytics begin by formulating questions for research and then collecting and using relevant data to find plausible answers. In contrast, techniques such as data mining collect large volumes of data and then explore what questions could be asked of this data by flagging different patterns. However, no prediction is perfect and outputs from both methods are limited to evidence found in the data. This is often why firms fall victim to sudden dramatic changes that could not have been predicted from past or current data.

Strategic Foresighting

Future outcomes may not be predictable because past and current data is limited to events that have already occurred. Choices made in the present help to shape what happens in the future. Therefore, managers developing plans for business renewal need to contemplate different pictures of the future in order to prepare the company in the event that perceived potential challenges or opportunities become a reality. A useful approach for this visionary planning is called strategic foresighting, defined as the process of thinking systematically about the future to inform decision-making in the present. The process of strategic foresighting involves

- identifying different scenarios of how the environment might evolve over time,
- anticipating the key factors that will drive change,

- deciding how to prepare now for different futures, and
- establishing contingency plans.

Figure 6.4 shows how the Gleaner Company may leverage strategic foresighting to cope with declining newspaper sales. The prospects may point to market diversification as the way forward. Effective foresighting involves thinking out of the box to contemplate even seemingly absurd scenarios. A combination of forecasting and foresighting can provide useful information to strengthen the strategic thrust of companies.

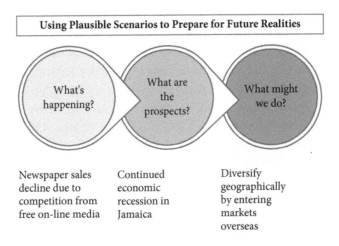

Using Plausible Scenarios to Prepare for Future Realities

What's happening? → What are the prospects? → What might we do?

| Newspaper sales decline due to competition from free on-line media | Continued economic recession in Jamaica | Diversify geographically by entering markets overseas |

Figure 6.4. A model of strategic foresighting at Gleaner Company

Improving Employee Morale

Employee morale refers to the emotion, attitude, satisfaction and outlook of persons within the organization. This sustainability component has a direct impact on a company's performance. Managers can build positive, empowering leader-employee relationships by providing support and encouragement in an environment of trust, mutual respect and confidence. Issues pertaining to employee competence should be resolved in partnership with affected employees, which may lead to counselling, coaching or reassignment. Employees should be given clear and specific expectations along with regular feedback. Managers should communicate transparently and effectively and provide incentives to promote team spirit and openness to new ideas.

To manage the business renewal process efficiently, a company must focus not only on its economic value but also on its organizational culture. As previously defined, organizational culture refers to the psychology, attitudes, experiences, beliefs and values emanating from the totality of people, systems and structures in place to implement strategies and tactics. A healthy culture promotes effective strategy execution through congruence across and within programmes, projects and routine activities. Managers can build a performance-oriented organizational culture by treating people like teammates rather than employees, acting on feedback from meaningful conversations and demonstrating genuine respect and care.

Managing Enterprise Risks

The current global economic crisis portends severe consequences for corporate Jamaica, such as decreased access to credit and weakened consumer demand. These conditions put risk management as a top priority in terms of anticipating and responding to outcomes that vary from expectations. Stockholders are inclined to use perceptions of risk to make investment decisions when a firm in which they hold shares reports a loss (Rockmore & Jone, 1996). However, stockholders are disadvantaged if they abandon a firm that later achieves turnaround or remains loyal only to witness business failure (Lawrence, 2004). In a turnaround situation, stockholders need to know how their perceptions of risk relate to the destiny of the troubled firm.

Aaker and Jacobson (1987) noted that risk has a substantial impact on business profitability. According to Capital Asset Pricing Theory, stockholders prefer investments having low variability in expected returns (Sharpe, 1964). This variability reflects the degree of risk, with increased variability corresponding to higher risk (Modigliani & Pogue, 1974). An empirical study by Lawrence (2004), conducted from 1969 to 2002, of firms listed on the Jamaica Stock Exchange revealed the following:

- Firms that achieve turnaround have lower levels of risk than those that do not.
- The firms that achieve turnaround have lower levels of risk at the recovery stage of the cycle compared to the decline stage.
- There is a negative association between the level of risk and firm performance during the decline stage of the turnaround cycle.
- There is a negative association between risk and performance for firms that do not achieve turnaround.

Increasing variability in earnings per share indicates a failing attempt at turnaround. Variability or risk reduction during the turnaround effort affords stakeholders a substantive signal that management has control of the situation. Yet, managers need to be mindful that too much focus on protecting the firm from downside risks or hazards can constrain pursuit of the upside risks or opportunities necessary for business turnaround and success.

A review of the strategies and financial performance of firms listed on the Jamaica Stock Exchange sheds light on this crucial issue. Of the forty-six firms that reported losses at some point during 1969 to 2002, only twenty-one recovered. None of the failed companies used expansion as a turnaround strategy, and most continued in their same lines of business. Interestingly, some of the successful firms broadened their scope of products or customers while others cut back the level of overall investment.

For example, beverage producer Desnoes and Geddes Limited and home furnishings retailer Courts Jamaica Limited experienced contrasting turnaround cycles during the economic recession in the late 1990s. Desnoes & Geddes, producers of Red Stripe beer, reduced exposure to downside risk by disinvesting in its soft drinks, wines and spirits business units to refocus on brewed products. On the other hand, Courts increased its exposure to upside risk by expanding its network of branches, product scope and warehousing space.

These observations suggest that managers should make risk-adjusted decisions on a contingency basis. This process involves

- identifying and quantifying the likelihood and potential impact of risk factors,
- agreeing the level of risk acceptable to each organization in terms of what is too much or too little,
- engaging stakeholders proactively to boost support for the organization, and
- executing prudent risk strategies such as avoidance, reduction, sharing and retention.

Workers Bank

Workers Savings and Loan Bank (Workers Bank) was launched as a company listed on the Jamaica Stock Exchange in 1973. The institution was established as a partnership between the Jamaican government, trade unions, credit unions and shareholders (Ricketts, 1995). Workers Bank succeeded the Government Savings Bank which was founded in 1870 and was the first commercial bank owned and operated entirely by Jamaicans. The institution was well capitalized at the start with oversubscription of its initial public offer of shares. The Government of Jamaica promoted Workers Bank as "a movement" for rapid progress of the people of Jamaica by giving them a further stake in the country in the post-colonial era.

Workers Bank facilitated deposits and withdrawals from over 540,000 small savers through facilities in 247 post office outlets across the country. This was the largest banking network in Jamaica and afforded access to the unbanked constituency. The government anticipated that Workers Bank would serve many generations of humble depositors. The institution was conceived as an instrument for worker participation in the financial services sector. The board of directors and senior management included several high profile politicians, civil servants, trade unionists and economists.

The Jamaican economy slipped into recession in 1974 due to shocks induced by the global oil crisis. Although revenues grew appreciably, Workers

Table 6.1. Workers Bank Financial Performance and Economic Climate (J$ million unless stated otherwise)

	1975	1980	1985	1990	1994	1996
Revenues	7.6	17.2	95.2	138.4	1,469.5	1,643.4
Net profit/(loss)	0.1	(3.9)	(7.8)	(39.1)	69.5	(454.8)
Total assets	81.6	164.5	571.2	791.1	6,356.0	8,945.2
Deposits	60.5	121.8	507.4	723.1	5,027.7	4,780.9
Loans	38.0	89.7	304.8	365.7	1,678.7	4,282.3
Shareholders' equity	0.7	(2.2)	1.8	(72.7)	230.3	(219.0)
Inflation rate (%)	17.4	28.2	26.0	22.0	35.0	26.1
Real GDP growth (%)	(0.3)	(5.8)	(4.6)	5.5	0.9	0.3
Treasury bill rate (%)	6.9	9.9	13.1	19.2	29.1	28.9
US dollar exchange rate (J$)	1.03	2.09	5.44	7.59	33.35	37.02

Source: Jamaica Stock Exchange yearbooks and Planning Institute of Jamaica annual reports.

Bank became insolvent by 1980 (table 6.1). By 1990, after years of losses, the bank had severe capital deficiency. Local media inferred that this dismal state of affairs arose from imprudent lending practices. In 1991, a small financial institution, Corporate Merchant Bank, made a successful bid to acquire Workers Bank through a combination of loans and private shares placement. This acquisition took place when the Government of Jamaica deregulated the local financial market, relinquishing controls on interest rates of capital accounts.

A new board of directors and new management were put in place to perform a strategic thrust that leveraged the large base of depositors and the post office network for increased visibility and access, particularly in deep rural areas. Management was aggressive in collecting amounts owed from delinquent clients, forcing some companies into bankruptcy. A new strategic plan was developed that emphasized cost leadership as well as service quality and delivery. The Workers Bank logo was redesigned and the company's logo, communications materials and facilities were designed to project two images: people empowerment and corporate power.

The bank launched several initiatives and new products. Saturday banking was re-introduced, the number of branches increased and a new back office technology commissioned. The Partner Plan allowed customers to save a specified minimum amount at regular intervals and then to receive the amount saved plus a bonus payment at the end of the period while also qualifying for entry to a grand draw at a later date. The "save as you spend" credit card annually returned to cardholders a percentage of the amount spent. Workers Bank also partnered with CS First Boston and International Energy Finance to execute a large private placement for Jamaica Private Power Company.

To motivate employees, Workers Bank developed a share ownership scheme, a scholarship programme, scheduled training to build required skills, an annual fun day and even bought twenty houses for staff members. Four of the seven senior managers and five of the eight department heads were women. The culture was shifted from a transactions oriented environment to an environment focused on sales and customer service. Employee promotions were based on merit not seniority.

In 1992, the bank acquired the assets and liabilities of the failed Bank of Credit and Commerce International (Overseas) Limited Jamaica branch. In 1993, the Workers Bank Visa Credit Card was launched with the rebate feature. The bank also opened its mid-west regional office and branches in Ocho Rios and Golden Grove.

By the end of 1994, Workers Bank had recovered from losses and financial distress, and management openly declared "mission accomplished" in the annual report.

The CEO attributed the success to company enlightenment from benchmarking global best practices, superior service quality, staff commitment and a sound technological platform (Workers Bank Annual Report, 1995). In addition to customer access by way of the post office network, the bank had twelve branches and seven sub-branches across the island. The annual report lamented the decline in interest rates on Government of Jamaica securities from 49 per cent to 29 per cent and announced its intention to become highly proactive in the foreign exchange market. Workers Bank also announced plans to place more emphasis on insurance premium financing and trust services.

In 1996, however, the bank again became capital deficient with a loss margin of 27 per cent of total revenues due to bad debts and overexposure in investments such as real estate and hotels, which were financed by high-cost short-term funds (figure 6.5). Workers Bank was just one of several indigenous financial institutions that collapsed in the 1990s, triggering intervention by the State in the form of the Financial Sector Adjustment Company (FINSAC), which was established to acquire majority ownership of failed entities and rehabilitate the sector for subsequent divestment (Chen-Young, 1998).

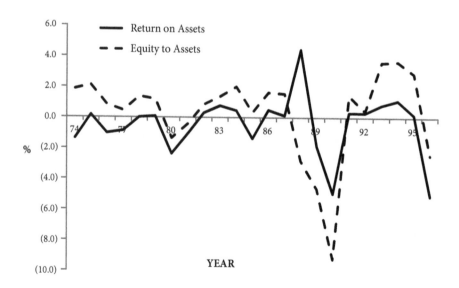

Figure 6.5. Losses and financial distress at Workers Bank
Source: Jamaica Stock Exchange yearbooks.

In 1990, the new owners of Workers Bank correctly diagnosed the severity and source of the declining performance. The bank was in a cash crisis because of internal weaknesses attributed to inappropriate lending practices. Based on the roadmap for business renewal (figure 1.3), the correct action for turnaround involves financial restructuring and efficiency improvement, which Workers Bank achieved in the early 1990s. Private placement of shares and a loan from the Eagle Merchant Bank stemmed the cash crisis and injected fresh capital. Improvements in efficiency arose from increasing the scale and scope of output, by way of new products and branch network expansion. New technologies and staff training initiatives were adopted for better utilization of physical and human resource inputs. However, managerial over-confidence in the bank's growth potential from the weakening Jamaica market caused performance relapse and subsequent dissolution.

Ultimately, this situation may have been avoided through strategic foresighting. Workers Bank relied on hindsight managerial techniques such as benchmarking to chart the way forward. However, the bank could have contemplated and prepared for different future scenarios such as rising customer bad debt based on current market factors like high interest rates. For its continued survival, Workers Bank should have also maintained higher levels of liquidity and capital reserves albeit at the expense of revenue growth.

Corporate Governance

Corporate governance refers to the systems and mechanisms used for directing company strategy, public accountability, policy formulation, and managerial decisions and actions. Corporate governance is at the heart of a company's reputation, integrity and image and becomes of particular importance in turnaround situations where delicate negotiations with diverse constituents are necessary. The rights of constituents must be respected, and matters pertaining to the status of the company must be disclosed in a timely and accurate manner.

Shareholders of Caribbean Steel, a prominent manufacturing company and a widely held stock on the Jamaica Stock Exchange, were shocked to learn that a consortium of local institutions had placed the company into receivership. The consortium's attorney declared that negotiations had been taking place for two years in efforts to recover amounts due. Further, the decision to place the company into receivership was a pre-emptive move after the consortium learned that one of Caribbean Steel's suppliers was about to file a judgement against the company. Furthermore, allegations of internal fraud led to the dismissal of the chief executive officer.

Good corporate governance establishes and communicates the roles and responsibilities of management transparently in order to eliminate any ambiguities. The chairman is expected to oversee the activities of the board of directors while the chief executive officer is responsible for running the business on a day-to-day basis. The board is expected to drive the business forward while ensuring prudent controls and adherence to a written code of conduct. While the board must be sensitive to immediate threats to business survival, it must maintain a long-term going concern perspective and keep abreast of relevant global and local trends and events.

Developing Small Business

To sustain profit recovery from decline, a small business must be managed based on its current stage in the industry life cycle. All goods and services will traverse the product life cycle unless deliberate steps are taken for product rejuvenation. Market demand and supply dynamics change as the industry moves from a start-up or embryonic stage, to growth, through to maturity and then decline. Small business managers need to scan the environment at regular intervals to detect signals of impending change.

During the start-up stage, prices and output are uncertain. Organizational learning is the key to prosperity. Ideas for new business opportunities arise from sources such as feedback from customers or changes in technology. Companies need to develop a sound business plan not only for attracting financial capital but also for focusing the enterprise on mission-critical activities. The *Global Entrepreneurship Monitor* (2010) reports that many small firms fail to transition from the start-up phase due to insufficient financing and imprudent decisions. Market research and well planned product launches are important for success at the start-up stage.

At the growth stage, industry demand outpaces supply which makes it possible for firms to expand output and increase prices to cope with inflation. A firm needs to have the required production, distribution and customer service systems in place in order to continue growing. Financing expansion endeavours can be a problem if a small firm does not have sufficient collateral. The Junior Market of the Jamaica Stock Exchange is one channel for accessing equity capital in Jamaica.

When a business enters the mature stage, expansion of output can be achieved if prices are low relative to the market. Product promotion becomes necessary to combat intensifying competition. Managers must also pay close attention to cost efficiency by assessing the supply chain, work processes and product mix. A firm may have opportunities to transition to new products emerging in the industry.

During decline, a company's product loses appeal and must be rejuvenated or replaced. A shakeout of firms in the industry may occur. Managers may be able to find profitable niche segments. Some companies build critical mass through strategic partnerships or mergers. A planned exit may be the best option if sales decline substantially.

Small firms in Jamaica also tend to rely heavily on pricing as the basis for competition. This can be fatal if the market demand is insufficient or a firm has supply constraints. Alternative strategies, such as superior customer service and product quality, should be exhausted as a first step for sales growth. Strategic partnerships to pool financial resources for better purchasing or promotion can result in large savings. Active membership in trade associations can also provide both a network of contacts for boosting sales and better access to financing options. Small business owners/managers need to leverage the Internet in order to keep abreast of industry developments and impending changes.

Conclusion

The preceding chapters of this book presented a user-friendly roadmap, showing four pathways for rescuing viable Jamaican businesses from losses and insolvency, and explained how to choose and navigate the correct pathway to suit each turnaround situation. Due to the high incidence of business failures throughout Jamaica's history and the paucity of holistic information for guiding managers, accessible and specific information regarding business renewal fills a research gap and provides a usable guide to turnaround in multiple contexts. Business renewal takes time to achieve and can occur even during periods of economic recession. The turnaround process is not only about generating economic value but also creating a "can do" organizational culture with sufficient team spirit, passion and excitement for business renewal projects.

The longer it takes incumbent management to admit decline and execute the right set of actions, the worse the situation becomes. While there is usually a period of warning before the company starts to suffer, early signals can be quite subtle. Managers need to be perceptive and use appropriate measures to scan external and internal environments for potential problems. Firms that have slack resources can cushion environmental jolts to buy time for turnaround. Small businesses, however, are quite vulnerable without this protective cushion. Managers should observe whether or not the source of decline is internal or external to the company in order to discern and apply the correct remedy. Business renewal is worth attempting if the going concern value of the business is substantially greater than its liquidation value.

Companies faced with a cash crisis must negotiate with creditors to reduce debt to an affordable level. In Jamaica, because of limited protection from the courts, managers must use private workouts to establish new arrangements for settling outstanding obligations. Debt rescheduling is a popular strategy for resolving financial distress, but this is unlikely to be sufficient for full relief. Companies also need to shrink the debt burden through other means such as asset retrenchment or sale of equity. For business renewal to occur, the cash budget needs to be zero-based with a tight control of accounts receivable and inventory where applicable. Because shareholders may become uneasy during cash crisis negotiations, companies should intentionally communicate with all involved.

Companies need to change strategy when the external environment causes decline. The roadmap in this book shows when to change corporate strategy and how to choose the correct method for deploying resources. The roadmap is particularly useful for small businesses because their resource constraints provide little room for error. Organizational agility is often necessary to quickly reconfigure the way resources and capabilities are combined to create and deliver new forms of value for stakeholders. A well-structured balanced scorecard strategy map and logical framework can keep the company focused on mission-critical activities for business renewal.

The balanced scorecard provides a clear picture of how a business model is intended to function in terms of organizational decisions and actions for creating and delivering stakeholder value. For a turnaround strategy to be successful, it must be compelling and driven by a coalition of influential stakeholders. Simple and transparent metrics should be used to drive strategy execution.

Irrespective of the situation, companies need to increase efficiency for turnaround by expanding organizational outputs relative to inputs, decreasing inputs relative to outputs or combining increased outputs and reduced inputs. A firm must also pay attention to changes in its break-even point which can increase when processes are automated. Process automation is permissible as long as revenue growth stays ahead of increased costs. Managers need to examine supply chains for opportunities to increase throughput, bearing in mind that a trade-off between operational efficiency and responsiveness to customers may be inevitable.

During profit recovery, managers should ensure that the sales growth rate is sustained within the limits of available financial resources. While demand forecasts are useful, managers should also exercise foresight by contemplating plausible future revenue and cost scenarios to better prepare for mitigating threats and seizing opportunities. Companies that derive revenues mainly from one industry should make adjustments in preparation for product maturation and changing market demand and supply dynamics.

The roadmap integrates international literature with Jamaican case studies in an effort to enable managers to prepare effective and efficient turnaround plans and reduce the likelihood of business failure during the process of business renewal. The case studies show that international prescriptions for business renewal are also relevant for Jamaica. In the local context, however, issues such as ongoing currency depreciation and high interest rates can greatly increase the amount of effort needed for business renewal.

There is scant literature about how to sustain profit recovery once turnaround is achieved. To clarify this aspect of business renewal, chapter 6 described how a combination of strategic forecasting and strategic foresighting can help managers to prepare the organization for future realities. Employee morale and enterprise risk management are also discussed as critical variables for preventing company relapse after turnaround.

Companies based in small island states, such as Jamaica, need to close performance gaps relative to global standards through business model transformation. Adjusted business models should work not only to rejuvenate organizational systems, capabilities and procedures, but also to develop special intangible resources, such as trust and reputation that are difficult to imitate or substitute. Through the development of these unique resources, firms can further their competitive advantage which will ultimately provide the stakeholder another form of support necessary for business renewal.

Firms must seek novel ways to develop and leverage their data assets for product innovation and enhanced customer service. Business intelligence refers to the analysis, presentation and delivery of critical information to managers for conceptualizing, creating, delivering and capturing stakeholder value. Companies often focus analyses on performance management in order to track processes and outcomes and use predictive analytics to anticipate future behaviours.

An implication of the roadmap for management scholars is that a combination of theories is required when describing how firms recover from declining profitability. From the perspective of Capital Asset Pricing Theory, risk has a substantial impact on firm profitability (Aaker & Johnson, 1987; Sharpe, 1964).

The resource-based view asserts that competitive advantage arises from superior skills in combining resources that are rare, inimitable and difficult to substitute (Peteraf, 1993. Wernerfelt, 1984; Penrose, 1959). Game Theory sees the firm as a player seeking to maximize payoffs by making rational and intelligent decisions aimed at outdoing competitors in the marketplace (Shapiro, 1989; Porter, 2008).

For management practice, the roadmap implies that firms need to have suitable human resource talent and commitment for effective and efficient strategy execution. Team members should not only have sufficient conceptual and technical skills, but also the interpersonal skills needed to build support teams and negotiate the terms for business renewal. Employee commitment, another key component of turnaround strategy execution and maintenance, comes from a sense of organizational belonging and ownership of the problem.

The history of firms listed on the Jamaica Stock Exchange confirms that organizational decline can happen even to the best of companies and in the best of circumstances. Managers in turnaround situations need to utilize the roadmap and prescriptions presented in this book in situations of decline. Case evidence has shown that the roadmap accounts for many different external environments. CMP Industries achieved turnaround in the aftermath of the global oil crises of the 1970s. Recovery at Courts Jamaica occurred during a period of high interest rates in the 1990s. Gleaner Company was rejuvenated amid the economic recession of 2007 to 2009. In conclusion, business renewal is about a frank assessment of the situation and decisive action by committed team players who are informed by relevant, timely and accurate data.

References

Adam, E. E., & Swamidass, P. M. (1989). Assessing operations management from a strategic perspective. *Journal of Management, 15*(2), 181–203.

Alderson, M. J., & Bekter, B. L. (1999). Assessing post-bankruptcy performance: An analysis of reorganized firms' cash flows. *Financial Management, 28*(2), 68–82.

Altman, E. I., & La Fleur, J. K. (1981). Managing a return to financial health. *Journal of Business Strategy, 2*(1), 31–31.

Argenti, J. (1976). *Corporate Collapse: The Causes and Symptoms.* New York, NY: Wiley.

Arogyaswamy, K., & Yasai-Ardekani, M. (1997). Organizational turnaround: Understanding the role of cutbacks, efficiency improvements, and investment in technology. *IEEE Transactions on Engineering Management, 44*(1), 3–11.

Aaker, D. A., & Jacobson, R. (1987). The role of risk in explaining differences in profitability . *Academy of Management Journal, 30*(2), 277–296.

Barker, V. L. III, & Duhaime, I. M. (1997). Strategic change in the turnaround process: Theory and empirical evidence. *Strategic Management Journal, 18*(1), 13–38.

Barker, V. L, & Mone, M. A. (1994). Retrenchment: Cause of turnaround or consequence of decline? *Strategic Management Journal, 15,* 395–405.

Barnard, C. I. (1938). *Functions of the Executive.* Cambridge, MA: Harvard University.

Beck, T., Demirguc-Kunt, A., & Maksimovic, V. (2008). Financing patterns around the world: Are small firms different? *Journal of Financial Economics, 89,* 467–487.

Bekter, B. L. (1995). An empirical examination of pre-packaged bankruptcy. *Financial Management, 24*(1), 3–22.

Bibeault, P. G. (1982). *Corporate Turnaround: How Managers Turn Losers Into Winners.* New York, NY: McGraw-Hill Book Company.

Bossidy, L., & Charan, R.(2002). *Execution: The Discipline of Getting Things Done.* New York, NY: Crown Business.

Bowman, E. H., & Singh, H. (1993). Corporate restructuring: Reconfiguring the firm. *Strategic Management Journal, 14,* 5–14.

Boyer, K. K., & Lewis, M. W. (2002). Competitive priorities: Investigating the need for trade-offs in operations strategy. *Production and Operations Management, 11*(1), 9–20.

Burns, T., & Stalker, G. M. (1961). *The Management of Innovation.* London: Tavistock.

Burvic, V., & Bartlett, W. (2003). Financial barriers to SME growth in Slovenia. *Economic and Business Review, 5*(3), 161–181.

Bushong, G. J., & Talbott, J. C. (1999). An application of the theory of constraints. *CPA Journal, 69*(4), 53–55.

Butler, J. W., Atkins, P. A., & Ivester, E. (2010). Managing in the "new normal": A self-help corporate governance program for directors and officers. *Navigating Today's Environment,* 45–51.

Cable & Wireless Jamaica Limited (LIME). Annual Report 2012.

Cameron, K. S., Kim, M. U., & Whetten, D. A. (1987). Organizational effects of decline and turbulence. *Administrative Science Quarterly, 32*(2), 222–240.

Caribbean Cement Limited. (2010). Consolidated Interim Financial Report for Nine Months Ended September 30, 2010.

Carter, R., & Van Auken, H. (2006). Small firm bankruptcy. *Journal of Small Business Management, 44*(4), 493–507.

Chatterjee, S., Dhillon, U. S., & Ramirez, G. G. (1996). Resolution of financial distress: Debt restructuring via Chapter 11, pre-packaged bankruptcies, and workouts. *Financial Management, 25*(1), 5–33.

Chen-Young, P. (1998). With all good intentions: Collapse of Jamaica's domestic financial sector. *Policy Papers on the Americas, 9,* study 12. November. CSIS Americas Program.

Cyert, R. M., & March, J. G. (1963). *A Behavioral Theory of the Firm.* Englewood Cliffs, NJ: Prentice Hall.

Ebben, J. J., & Johnson, A. C. (2005). Efficiency, flexibility, or both? Evidence linking strategy to performance in small firms. *Strategic Management Journal, 26*(13), 249–254.

Elliott, D. R., & Palmer, R. (2008). Institutions and Caribbean economic performance: Insights from Jamaica. *Studies in Comparative International Development, 43,* 181–205.

Finkelstein, C. (1993). Financial distress as a noncooperative game: A proposal for overcoming obstacles to private workouts. *Yale Law Journal, 102*(8), 2205–2227.

Francis, J. D., & Desai, A. B. (2005). Situational and organizational determinants of turnaround . *Management Decision, 43*(9), 1203–1224.

Gilson, S. C. (1989). Management turnover and financial distress. *Journal of Financial Economics, 25*, 241–262.

Gilson, S. C. (1990). Bankruptcy, boards, banks, and bondholders. *Journal of Financial Economics, 27*, 355–387.

Gilson, S. C., John, K., & Lang, L. H. P. (1990). Troubled debt restructurings: An empirical study of private reorganization of firms in default. *Journal of Financial Economics, 27*, 315–326.

Global Entrepreneurship Monitor. (2010). *2009 Jamaica Report*. University of Technology, Jamaica.

Goldratt, E. M. (1997). *Critical Chain*. Barrington, MA: North River Press.

Gopinath, C. (1991). Turnaround: Recognizing decline and initiating intervention. *Long Range Planning, 24*(6), 96–101.

Gopinath, C. (1995). Bank strategies toward firms in decline. *Journal of Business Venturing, 10*, 75–92.

Gopinath, C. (2005). Recognizing decline: The role of triggers. *American Journal of Business, 20*(1), 21–27.

Grinyer, P., & McKiernan, P. (1990). Generating major change in stagnating companies. *Strategic Management Journal, 11*, 131–146.

Hambrick, D. C., & D'Aveni, R. A. (1988). Large corporate failures as downward spirals. *Administrative Science Quarterly, 33*, 1–23.

Hansen, C. D., & Salerno, T. J. (1991). A pre-packaged bankruptcy strategy. *Journal of Business Strategy*, January/February 36–41.

Harker, M., & Sharma, B. (2000). Leadership and the company turnaround process. *The Leadership & Organization Development Journal. 21*(1), 36–47.

Hashi, I. (1997). The economics of bankruptcy, reorganization, and liquidation. *Russian and East European Finance and Trade, 33*(4), 6–34.

Hayes, R. H., & Upton, D. M. (1998). Operations-based strategy. *California Management Review, 40*(4), 8–25.

Higgins, R. C. (1977). How much growth can a company afford? *Financial Management, 6*(3), 7–16.

Isaac, S., & Michael, W. B. (1990). *Handbook in Research and Evaluation*. Second edition. San Diego, CA: Edits Publishers.

Isern, J., Meaney, M. C., & Wilson, S. (2010). Corporate transformation under pressure. Retrieved from http://www.mckinsey.com/insights/organization/corporate_transformation_under_pr.

Jamaica Stock Exchange. (2011). Company reports. Retrieved from http://www.jamstockex.com.

Jamaica Stock Exchange. (2012). Company reports. Retrieved from http://www.jamstockex.com.

Jog, V. M., Kotlyar, I., & Tate, D. G. (1993). Stakeholder losses in corporate restructuring: Evidence from four cases in the North American Steel Industry. *Financial Management, 22*(3), 185–201.

Kaplan, K. S., & Norton, D. P. (1992). *Balanced Scorecard*. Boston, MA: Harvard Business School Publishing.

Laitinen, E. (2011). Effect of reorganization actions on the financial performance of small entrepreneurial distressed firms. *Journal of Accounting and Organizational Change, 7*(1), 57–95.

Lawrence, P., & Lorsch, J. (1967). *Organization and Environment*. Homewood, IL.: Richard D. Irwin, Inc.

Lawrence, W. W. (1995). Business turnaround and organizational slack : An empirical investigation. (Doctoral dissertation). Nova Southeastern University, Florida.

Lawrence, W. W. (2004). Using risk to anticipate firm turnaround. *Business Review, Cambridge, 1*(2), 115–118.

Lawrence, W. W. (2007/8). Small business operations strategy: Aligning resources and priorities. *Journal of Small Business Strategy, 18*(2), 89–103.

Lawrence, W. W. (2011). Correcting for the future. *Industrial Engineer, 43*(5), 26–31.

Lawrence, W. W. (2012). Coping with external pressures: A note on SME strategy. *Social and Economic Studies, 61*(1), 161–170.

Lawrence, W. W., & Abrikian, H. S. (2013). SME restructuring: Financial strategies for turnaround and growth. Paper presented at the Fifteenth International Academy of Management Conference in Lisbon, Portugal.

Lawrence, W. W., & Jones, J. P. (2001). Business turnaround: Resolving financial distress. *Journal of Applied Management and Entrepreneurship, 6*(1), 105–120.

Lorange, P., & Nelson, R. T. (1987). How to recognize and avoid organizational decline. *Sloan Management Review, 28*(3), 41–48.

Lowson, R. H. (2005), Retail operations strategies: Empirical evidence of role, competitive contribution, and life cycle. *International Journal of Operations and Production Management, 25*(7/8), 642–680.

McConnell, J., & Servaes, H. (1991). The economics of pre-packaged bankruptcy. *Journal of Applied Corporate Finance*, Summer, 93–97.

Miles, R. H. (2010). Accelerating corporate transformations (Don't lose your nerve). *Harvard Business Review*, Reprint R1001C (January–February), 2–8.

Mintzberg, H. (1994). *The Rise and Fall of Strategic Planning*. New York, NY: Free Press.

Modigliani, F., & Pogue, G. A. (1974). An introduction to risk and return. *Financial Analysts Journal*, March–April, *30*, 68–80.

Moulton, W. N., & Thomas, H. (1993). Bankruptcy as a deliberate strategy: Theoretical considerations and empirical evidence. *Strategic Management Journal, 14*, 125–135.

Musczyk, J. P., & Steel, R. P. (1998). Leadership style and the turnaround executive. *Business Horizons, 41*(2), 39–46.

O'Neill, H. M. (1986a.) An analysis of the turnaround strategy in commercial banking. *Journal of Management Studies, 23*, 165–188.

O'Neill, H. M. (1986b). Turnaround and recovery. What strategy do you need? *Long Range Planning, 19*(1), 80–88.

Pearce II, J. A. (2007). The value of corporate financial measures in monitoring downturn and managing turnaround : An exploratory study. *Journal of Management Issues, 19*(2), 253–270.

Penrose, E. T. (1959). *The Theory of the Growth of the Firm.* Oxford: Basil Blackwell.

Peteraf, M. A. (1993). The cornerstones of competitive advantage: A resource-based view. *Strategic Management Journal, 14*, 179–191.

Planning Institute of Jamaica. (2006). *Economic and Social Survey Jamaica 2005.*

Planning Institute of Jamaica. (2010). *Economic and Social Survey Jamaica 2009.*

Planning Institute of Jamaica. (2012). *Economic and Social Survey Jamaica 2011.*

Planning Institute of Jamaica. (2013). *Economic and Social Survey Jamaica 2012.*

Porter, M. E. (2008). *On Competition.* Boston, MA: Harvard Business Press.

Ramanujam, V. (1984). Environmental context, organizational context, strategy and corporate turnaround: An empirical investigation. (Doctoral dissertation). University of Pittsburgh, Pennsylvania.

Ricketts, M. (1995). Workers Bank at 21: The promise of more exciting things to come. *Money Index*, 17 January, 13–42.

Robbins, D. K. and Pearce II, J. A. (1992). Turnaround: retrenchment and recovery. *Strategic Management Journal, 18*(4), 599–620.

Rockmore, B. W., & Jone, F. F. (1996). Business investment strategy and firm performance: A comparative examination of accounting and market-based measures. *Managerial Finance, 22*(8), 44–56.

Salazar, A. L., Soto, R. C., & Mosqueda, R. E. (2012). The impact of financial decisions and strategy on small business competitiveness. *Global Journal of Business Research, 6*(2), 93–103.

Schendel, D., & Patton, G. (1976). Corporate Stagnation and Turnaround. *Journal of Economics and Business, 28*, 236–241.

Schendel, D., Patton, G., & Riggs, J. (1976). Corporate turnaround strategies: A study of profit decline and recovery. *Journal of General Management, 3*, 3–11.

Senge, P. (1990). *The Fifth Discipline: The Art and Practice of the Learning Organization.* New York, NY: Doubleday.

Shapiro, C. (1989). The theory of business strategy. *The Rand Journal of Economics 20*(1), 125–137.

Sharpe, W. F. (1964). Capital asset prices: A theory of market equilibrium under conditions of risk. *Journal of Finance, 19*, 425–442.

Shrader, M. J., & Hickman, K. A. (1993). Economic issues in bankruptcy and reorganization. *Journal of Applied Business Research, 9*(3), 110–134.

Silva, A. P., & Santos, C. M. (2012). Financial and strategic factors associated with the profitability and growth of SME in Portugal. *International Journal of Economics and Finance, 4*(3), 46–60.

Singh, J. V. (1986). Performance, slack and risk taking in organizational decision making. *Academy of Management Journal, 29*(3), 562–585.

Simon, H. A. (1957). *Administrative Behavior.* New York, NY: Free Press.

Smith, A. (1977). *An Inquiry into the Nature and Causes of the Wealth of Nations.* Chicago, IL: University of Chicago Press.

Smith, S. & Graves, C. (2005). Corporate turnaround and financial distress. *Managerial Auditing Journal, 20*(3), 304–320.

Snyder, R. H. (1999). How I reengineered a small business. *Strategic Finance, 80*(11), 26–30.

Sum, C., Kow, S., & Chen, C. (2004). A taxonomy of operations strategies of high performing small and medium enterprises in Singapore. *International Journal of Operations and Production Management, 24*(3/4), 321–348.

Taylor, F. W. (1911). *The Principles of Scientific Management.* New York, NY: Norton Library/Harper & Row (1967).

Teece, D. J., Pisano, G., & Shuen, A. (1997). Dynamic capabilities and strategic management. *Strategic Management Journal, 18*(7), 509–533.

Thain, D. H., & Goldthorpe, R. L. (1989a). Turnaround management: Recovery strategies. *Business Quarterly, 54*(1), 55–62.

Thain, D. H., & Goldthorpe, R. L. (1989b). Turnaround management: Causes of decline. *Business Quarterly, 54*(1), 55–62.

Weilemaker, M. W., Elfring, T., & Volberda, H. W. (2000). Strategic renewal in large European firms: Investigating viable trajectories of change. *Organization Development Journal, 18*(4), 49–68.

Weiss, L. A. (1990). Bankruptcy resolution: Direct costs and violation of priority claims. *Journal of Financial Economics, 27*, 285–314.

Weitzel, W., & Jonsson, E. (1989). Decline in organizations: A literature integration and extension. *Administrative Science Quarterly, 34*(1), 91–109.

Welsh, J. A., & White, J. F. (1981). A small business is not a little big business. *Harvard Business Review, 59*(4), 18–27.

Wernerfelt, B. (1984). A resource based view of the firm. *Strategic Management Journal, 5*(2), 171–180.

White, M. J. (1983). Bankruptcy costs and the new bankruptcy code. *Journal of Finance, 28*, 477–488.

Workers Bank. (1995). Mission accomplished. *1994 Annual Report.*

Wruck, K. H. (1990). Financial distress, reorganization, and organizational efficiency. *Journal of Financial Economics, 27*, 419–444.

Index

CPSIA information can be obtained
at www.ICGtesting.com
Printed in the USA
LVHW010916230222
711732LV00004B/771

9 789766 404987